# LOMOND GUIDE TO THE
# BIRDS
### *of the*
# BRITISH ISLES

# Lomond Guide to the
# BIRDS
### *of the*
# British Isles

Elizabeth Balmer

# LOMOND

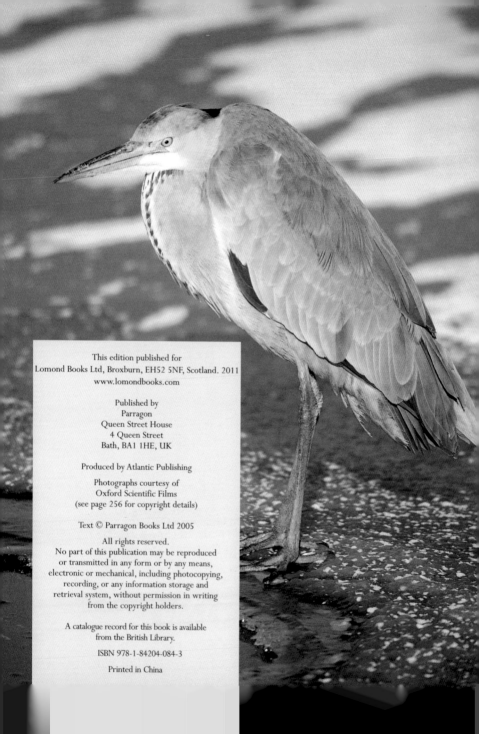

This edition published for
Lomond Books Ltd, Broxburn, EH52 5NF, Scotland. 2011
www.lomondbooks.com

Published by
Parragon
Queen Street House
4 Queen Street
Bath, BA1 1HE, UK

Produced by Atlantic Publishing

Photographs courtesy of
Oxford Scientific Films
(see page 256 for copyright details)

Text © Parragon Books Ltd 2005

A catalogue record for this book is available
from the British Library.

ISBN 978-1-84204-084-3

Printed in China

# CONTENTS

# INTRODUCTION

T he pursuit of finding and identifying birds is an ideal way to get back in touch with nature, to move away from the stressful and trivial worries of modern life. Birds can be an endless source of delight and are to be seen everywhere. Birdwatching, for many people, is an enjoyment, something that can easily be done on a casual basis and with the minimum of equipment. The birds chosen for this guide represent those that are either resident in Britain or are frequent visitors. Of course, many hundreds of species visit the British Isles as they migrate across the globe, but the selection made here is of those that the amateur enthusiast is most likely to encounter.

Being able to identify an individual species with confidence gives a great sense of satisfaction. This book has many features that will help anyone interested in nature make an informed identification of most of the birds to be found in Britain. The details offered, together with the pictures, supply brief but useful information. The description provides a clear guide to the physical details of a bird, both at rest and in flight. Behaviour can often be a useful help to identification, so some information on this is also given where it is relevant. The variety of noises made is often a vital means of telling one bird from another, particularly when related birds can be so alike physically. Of course, it is always difficult to describe a particular sound in writing! Habitats change over time, along with changes in the environment, and the information here aims to be up to date. Many summer or winter visitors change their habitat depending on which country they are currently in; their British habitat is the one given here. Details on nesting are brief and general, as many birds produce more than one brood in a season and it is difficult to be precise about exactly how many eggs are laid.

## Identifying Birds

The best time to look for most birds is early in the morning, when they tend to be more active – and, for some species, also in the early evening. However, it is possible to see a few birds throughout the day, particularly hawks and other birds that soar high in the sky. Birdwatching is an all-year-round activity, since different species are seen at different times of the year. Although even the garden or local park will usually have some interesting birds to watch, quite similar types of birds often prefer widely differing habitats, so try to look in a variety of places. The main field marks – physical characteristics that can be picked out in the wild – are often used in the descriptions. These are as clear as possible but sometimes using a technical term is unavoidable, although this has been kept to a minimum. The exact parts of a bird that these terms refer to are shown on the photograph on page 13. Many birds have different breeding plumages, or the males have different colouring to the females, and as much detail as possible about this has been given. However, juvenile birds, faded adults late in summer – and sometimes moulting birds – can often look very odd and be extremely hard to identify. Each bird is also an individual, so it may not match the pictures in this book exactly. It is therefore important to concentrate on shape and pattern rather than specific markings, and to use more than one field mark to identify each bird.

## Size

Size is another important factor – if an all-black bird is only glimpsed fleetingly, its size will tell you immediately if it is more likely to be a member of the blackbird family or one of the much bigger crows. At first, it may be difficult to estimate size at a distance, but constant practice will help.

## Habitat

The kind of habitat that a bird prefers may also be a big clue to identifying a particular species. Habitat is also important because many birds can only thrive in certain conditions, so it is essential that their habitat is protected or the species may die out.

## Common and Scientific Names

Different species of birds are organized into families that have the same characteristics. Some families have only a few members while others have many. In addition, each individual bird not only has a common name, but also a Latin scientific name. The first part of this is known as the genus, and indicates a group within a family that is closely related. The second part identifies a particular bird. Sometimes a bird will have a third part to its Latin name, which identifies a sub-species, but the differences cannot usually be easily identified in the wild. One advantage of Latin names is that they are the same in any language, so birdwatchers all over the world can recognize the same bird.

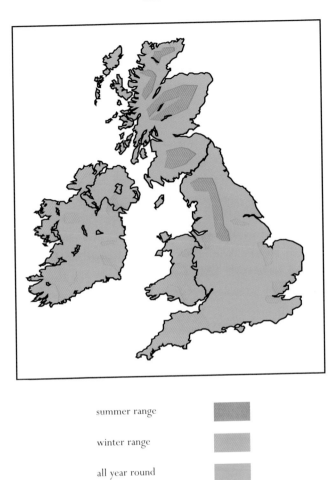

summer range

winter range

all year round

## Range Maps

The same birds are not found everywhere, and some are only found in certain areas at specific times. Each bird pictured in this book has a range map, which is colour-coded to show when it is most likely to be seen. Although birds do wander out of their set ranges and storms sometimes blow them off course during migration, the maps will show the most likely candidates within a particular area.

## Classification

The birds are set in the order of the families to which they belong. Traditionally, the most primitive birds are at the beginning and the most highly developed at the end. Birds that are extremely rare or are only casual visitors to the British Isles have been omitted – unless they are locally very common.

## Birdwatching Ethics and Conservation

Birdwatchers must be very aware of their behaviour when out watching – and this is becoming even more essential as more and more people take it up. Always bear in mind that the welfare of the bird must be more important than any other consideration and avoid causing any kind of disturbance – particularly when the birds are nesting or roosting. Never do anything that might compromise the habitat of a bird. Several birds have disappeared purely because their habitat has been damaged or destroyed by human intervention. Bird feeders will bring many species right into the garden, but it is important to keep them scrupulously clean to avoid spreading diseases through the bird population.

It is also polite, and will help others coming along later, if the rights of landowners and other people are considered and observed. Never trespass or cause any damage to private property.

## Keeping Track of Sightings

Most birdwatchers like to keep a record of the birds they have seen. Rather than just ticking off the names on a list, many keep a notebook recording the name of the bird, the date and place, and information about its habits and field marks. If a rare bird is spotted, this data will be essential in order to have the sighting verified. Rare birds are not only seen by experts – informed amateurs have just as much chance of seeing one if they are well-prepared and know what to look for. Knowing what to expect is also important; before visiting a new area, check what species are likely to be found there.

Many local and national bird organizations work to preserve important habitats that are under threat and to protect individual species, and amateurs can usually become involved. It is also often worth contacting these organizations since they will be able to offer information on good observation places. However, don't become too involved in how others think birdwatching should be done; it should always be enjoyable, so the best approach is always the one that suits you.

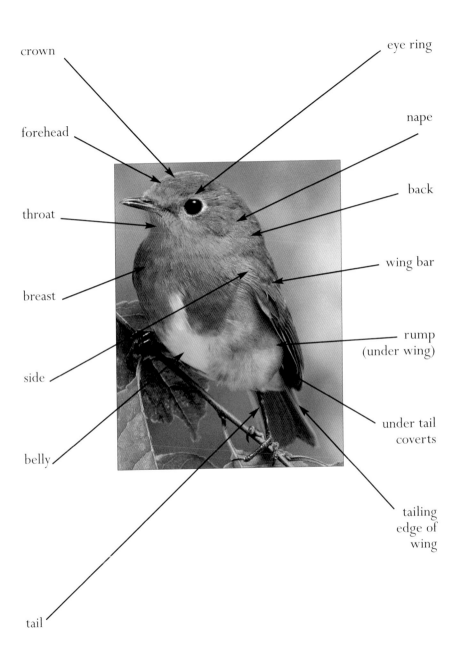

crown

eye ring

forehead

nape

throat

back

breast

wing bar

side

rump
(under wing)

belly

under tail
coverts

tailing
edge of
wing

tail

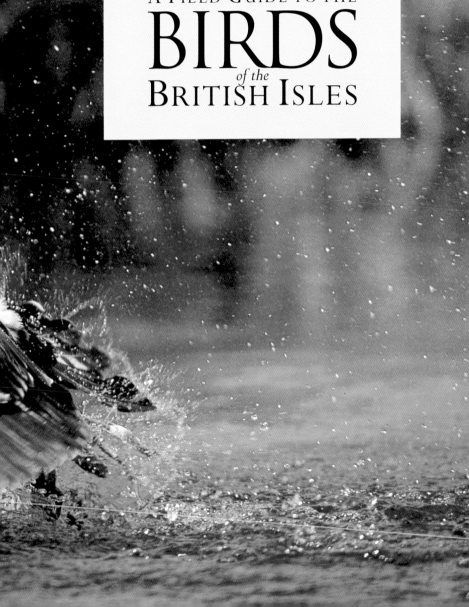

A FIELD GUIDE TO THE
# BIRDS
*of the*
## BRITISH ISLES

# RED-THROATED DIVER (GAVIA STELLATA)

**VOICE** During summer it emits a long, high-pitched wailing sound. In winter its call is harsher, a rapidly repeated cawing often heard in flight.

**HABITAT** Prefers small lakes, lochs and ponds in the north for breeding although it needs to fly to coastal areas in search of food. In winter, mainly coastal, but can be found inland on lakes.

**NESTING** Dark olive-brown eggs are laid in pairs within a grass-lined depression or scrape at the waterside.

**RANGE** Breeds in northern Europe, Iceland and Scandinavia, migrates further south along western coastal stretches and some inland rivers and lakes in eastern Europe.

More common than its relatives the black-throated and the great northern divers, the red-throated diver is a slimmer, elegant bird with its characteristically upwards-tilted head and bill. In summer, during the breeding season, it bears a bright red throat patch; with its blue-grey face and side plumage, the throat patch can appear black at a distance. Its upper parts are grey-brown, changing to dark grey with white spots in winter which can also make it difficult to distinguish from the black-throat, though generally its plumage is paler. Although clumsy on land, it is an expert diver and remains underwater for lengthy periods searching for fish. Length: 53-68cm.

# (GAVIA ARCTICA) BLACK-THROATED DIVER

A slightly larger and stockier diver than its red-throated cousin, the black-throat is distinguished by its thicker, straighter bill. In winter its plumage is mainly black upper parts with white below and its head lacks the white eye ring seen on the red-throat. During the summer the black-throat's head and neck are grey-blue, with striking white stripes on its neck that serve to emphasize its black throat. Its black upper parts and wings are adorned with a chequerboard of white spots and stripes. It carries a sharply contrasting white patch on its flank at all times, which is often visible at water level. Length approx: 55-73cm.

**VOICE** Mostly silent during winter and in flight. During breeding its call is a long, mournful cawing and wailing with some pulsating croaking.

**HABITAT** Prefers larger upland lakes which provide rich sources of fish and molluscs, requiring less flying in search of food. During winter can be found in coastal areas.

**NESTING** Shallow waterside scrapes, often found on islets, containing 2 black-blotched, olive-brown eggs.

**RANGE** Breeds in north-western Scotland, Scandinavia, northern Russia and Iceland, moving down to Black Sea and Mediterranean areas.

# GREAT NORTHERN DIVER (GAVIA IMMER)

Larger than both the red-throat and the
black-throat, the great northern diver has a
thick, powerful neck and a heavy, straight bill.
In summer, its upper part plumage is not too
different from that of the black-throated
diver, with striking black and white
chequerboard markings; however, its bill,
head and neck are almost totally black, with a
necklace and throat band of white stripes.
During the winter its underparts are paler
with its white face extending around the eye.
Its upper parts are also paler, as is its bill, and
it is distinguished from other divers by its
heavier build and its steeper forehead.
Length: 27-36cm.

# (TACHYBAPTUS RUFICOLLIS) LITTLE GREBE

The little grebe is the smallest grebe, with a rounded body and short neck giving it a dumpy appearance. During the breeding season it has dark brown plumage on its upper parts and fluffy white feathers on its rear end. Its chestnut cheeks and front neck are distinguishing characteristics, as is the pale yellow streak at the base of the bill. In winter, the little grebe is paler all over, losing the colouring on the neck and cheeks, with a whitish throat and darker brown cap. In flight it shows white patches on its wings which are lost in winter. Its shape and shorter bill distinguish it from other grebes at that time. Length approx: 27cm.

**VOICE** Loud, whinnying call.

**HABITAT** Slow-flowing rivers, canals, ponds, freshwater lakes, reservoirs and gravel pits. Can be found on coastal estuaries out of breeding season.

**NESTING** On floating vegetation attached to overhanging branches or aquatic plants; lays 4–6 white eggs.

**RANGE** Breeds across central and southern Europe; can be found as far south as sub-Saharan Africa.

# GREAT CRESTED GREBE
## (PODICEPS CRISTATUS)

The great crested grebe is an elegant bird, with a long thin neck and ornate head plumes. These were greatly sought after in the nineteenth century which led to near extinction. The plumes are absent during the winter, leaving a dark cap. The crest is black and the prominent ear tufts are chestnut with black tips. The upper parts are grey-brown and the underparts and neck are predominantly white. Its face is white, with white above the eye, and its bill is long and pink. It dives to feed and to escape, although it does fly readily. Its feet are placed far back on its body which can make it appear clumsy on land. Great crested grebes have an impressive and elaborate courtship display consisting of simultaneous head shaking with crests erect and a mutual collection and presentation of weeds caught in their bills. Length approx: 46-50cm.

**Voice** Rumbling growls, barks and clicks.
**Habitat** Large freshwater lakes, canals, gravel pits and slow rivers. During winter can be found in coastal areas.
**Nesting** Builds a nest on a pile of floating vegetation in shallow reed-fringed water; 3–6 eggs are laid. Very young grebes often ride on their parents' backs.
**Range** Across most of Europe, avoiding colder north.

# MANX SHEARWATER (PUFFINUS PUFFINUS)

**VOICE** Silent at sea. Wailing and screaming on the nest.

**HABITAT** Oceanic, except during breeding when found on remote islands and mainland cliff tops in large colonies.

**NESTING** A single white egg, placed in grass-lined burrow or crevice.

**RANGE** Iceland, Faroe Islands and northern Britain; can migrate across Atlantic as far as South America.

The plumage of the shearwater can vary geographically, but the Atlantic Manx shearwater is clearly black and white. It has black upper parts, back of neck and head, and contrasting white underparts, including white under the wing. This contrast of black and pure white is most apparent in flight. More southern varieties lack this vivid colouring and tend to be slightly browner. A smaller bird than other shearwaters, it has long slim wings. It is a frequent swimmer and in flight tends to glide, beating its wings occasionally. It does not follow ships. It only comes to shore at night and breeds in colonies. Length: 30-38cm.

# (FULMARUS GLACIALIS) FULMAR

A large, stocky seabird, the fulmar is related to the albatross. It has a white head, neck and white underparts, with a blue-grey back, wings and tail. The neck is short and thick and the wings show some white plumage in flight. The short, thick bill is yellow, with tube-like nostrils on the top. Northern fulmars are a darker grey, with dark grey wing tips. The fulmar flies low with stiff wings and shallow wing beats, expertly gliding and banking. When defending their nests, they spit out a foul-smelling regurgitated liquid. Spending most of their time out at sea, fulmars are sociable birds, with flocks often seen following ships in the hope of food. Length: 45-50cm.

**VOICE** Chuckling when on cliffs, cackling calls at sea.
**HABITAT** Always offshore, except when breeding; coastal cliffs and occasionally on buildings.
**NESTING** A single white egg laid on bare rock.
**RANGE** Breeds across northern Atlantic and North Sea. Can be found on Scottish coastline, especially on the Northern Isles.

# GANNET
(SULA BASSANA)

The largest British seabird, adult gannets have bright white, cigar-shaped bodies with characteristic black wing tips. The wings are long and narrow and the tail is long and pointed. During the breeding season the adult has a yellow wash over its head and the back of its neck. Juveniles are brownish, speckled with white. They acquire their adult feathers by moulting over five years, gradually becoming more pied until they are completely white. Both adults and juveniles have long necks, black legs, webbed feet and long sharp beaks. They fly low over the water and feed by flying high, circling and then plunging into the sea with their wings folded back. Length: 86-94cm.

**VOICE** Silent at sea. Cackling calls at nest.
**HABITAT** Breeds in large colonies on remote islands, flat topped stacks, ledges and sheer coastal cliffs. Winters out at sea.
**NESTING** A single white egg incubated by both parents in a pile of seaweed.
**RANGE** Found across northern Atlantic, migrating south towards Africa.

# CORMORANT
(PHALACROCORAX CARBO)

The cormorant is a large aquatic bird with a long neck and tail. Its plumage is mainly black and at close range can appear to have an oily sheen. Juvenile cormorants are brown with white underparts. The adult has white cheeks and chin and an orange patch below its eye. A white patch can be seen on the cormorant's thighs in summer. Its yellowish bill is long and hooked. It has large, black, webbed feet, useful for swimming both on the surface and underwater in search of fish. It flies with its neck extended and its head held slightly upright, and groups often fly in a 'v' formation. Can be seen perched with its wings held out to dry. Length: 80-100cm.

**Voice** Silent at sea. Noisy croaking at nest.
**Habitat** Coastal cliffs and rocky islands. Some colonies inland in trees by lakes and reservoirs.
**Nesting** Nests are lined with either seaweed or grass and situated on cliffs or in trees. On isolated islands they can be found on the ground. 3-5 pale blue eggs.
**Range** Found around coast of Britain, although less common in the south east. Breeds throughout Europe and northern Atlantic.

# SHAG (PHALACROCORAX ARISTOTELIS)

**Voice** Mostly silent. Croaks during breeding.

**Habitat** Mainly coastal, rarely venturing inland. Will nest in colonies on ledges and sea cliffs or among large boulders.

**Nesting** 3 pale blue eggs laid in a pile of seaweed and incubated by both parents.

**Range** Found throughout north of Britain and on the western coasts. Breeds across nothern Europe and Atlantic down to western Mediterranean.

The shag is smaller than the cormorant but similar in appearance. It is slender with a long neck and tail and a long, thin bill which also sports a yellow base. Black all over with a green, oily sheen during the breeding season, the shag develops a short forward-curving crest on the front of its steep forehead. Its eyes are a pale blue-green. The shag can be distinguished from the cormorant by the lack of white on its head and thighs. Juvenile shags are brown with lighter brown underparts. A confident diver, it can stay underwater for lengthy periods pursuing fish.
Length: 65-80cm.

# (BOTAURUS STELLARIS) BITTERN

A shy and well camouflaged heron, the bittern is rarely seen. It is a large, thick-set, dumpy marsh bird. When resting and walking it can appear hunched, but when alarmed it stands frozen and upright, stretching its neck and holding its sharp bill vertically skyward. Its plumage is tawny brown, mottled and streaked with white and black bars, which enables it to hide in reed beds. It flies reluctantly, with broad, rounded wings and trailing green feet. Its dependence on reed beds makes it a threatened species, with very few pairs left in the UK at the time of writing. Length: 70-80cm.

**Voice** Loud booming call sometimes carrying for over a mile.
**Habitat** Marshland with reed beds, gravel pits and rivers, and other areas of open water with thick vegetation.
**Nesting** Three to four green-blue eggs laid on a platform of reeds and vegetation on the ground or in shallow water.
**Range** Breeds across Europe and Asia.

# GREY HERON
## (ARDEA CINEREA)

The grey heron is the largest and most widespread European heron. It has a slender body with a long bill, neck and legs. Its head and neck are white with a black crest of feathers, and a black streak on its foreneck and breast. Its upper parts are blue-grey and its underparts are grey-white. In flight its wings are broad and rounded with contrasting black flight feathers. The grey heron's bill is yellow and dagger-like and its legs are brown. Often seen stalking its food in shallow water or on banks, with its neck extended. In flight, its head and neck are tucked back in typical heron fashion and its wings flap slowly.
Length: 90-98cm.

**VOICE** A loud harsh call.
**HABITAT** Shallow water, both fresh and salt. Inland lakes, gravel pits, marshes, estuaries and shores. Will visit garden ponds and fish farms.
**NESTING** Breeds in tall trees and on cliff edges near to fish supplies. Sometimes solitary but usually found in colonies.
**RANGE** Found throughout Europe; can winter in Africa.

# MUTE SWAN
## (CYGNUS OLOR)

The commonest swan in Britain, the mute swan is a large and distinctive bird. It has pure white plumage, black legs and feet, and a distinctive red-orange concave bill with black knob and base. It holds its long neck in a characteristic 's'-shaped curve with its bill gracefully pointing downwards. When swimming, its tail is often turned up and its wings partially raised over its back. It flies with regular, slow wing beats and its neck outstretched. The juvenile is brown feathered, with an almost pink bill. Although mostly communal, pairs can be aggressively territorial during breeding. Can live for up to 24 years.
Length: 145-160cm.

**VOICE** Mostly silent. Hisses when angry. Wings make throbbing sound when flying.
**HABITAT** Variety of freshwater sites: shallow lakes, slow-flowing rivers, canals. Sheltered shorelines and estuaries. Urban parks.
**NESTING** 5-7 pale, greenish eggs laid in large nests of sticks, reeds and feathers in shallows at the water's edge.
**RANGE** Widespread in Europe towards Russia and Black Sea.

# WHOOPER SWAN (CYGNUS CYGNUS)

**Voice** Noisiest of swans, it trumpets when flying.

**Habitat** Feeds in shallows; roosts on open water. Lakes, coastal estuaries, bogs and flooded fields.

**Nesting** Builds huge mounds of vegetation, often on islands. Lays 5-6 white eggs which are incubated by the female.

**Range** Breeds in Iceland, Arctic waters and northern Atlantic. Visits northern Europe, including Scotland and Ireland and parts of eastern England.

A winter visitor to Britain, the whooper swan is very similar to the mute swan, but with some key differences. It has a more triangular bill which is black and yellow. The tip and base of the bill is black and the yellow wedge extends towards the eye. It holds its long thin neck straight and its head erect, and its head has quite a flat profile. The juvenile whooper is more grey than the juvenile mute and its bill is pink and grey. It can often be seen flying in flocks, frequently in a chevron formation, although it is a solitary bird during the breeding season. Length: 145-160cm.

# (CYGNUS BEWICKII) BEWICK'S SWAN

Bewick's swan is a winter visitor and the smallest British swan. Like both the mute swan and the whooper, its plumage is pure white; however, its bill is blacker. The bill also has a yellow base, but with less yellow than on the whooper swan, since it barely reaches the nostrils. It also has a shorter neck and its head is more rounded than the whooper swan's. Juvenile Bewick's are a pinkish grey colour with a pink bill. Bewick's swans tend not to fly in formation and their wings are quiet, unlike the mute swan.
Length: 115-125cm.

**VOICE** Honks in flight. Quietly babbles when feeding.

**HABITAT** In winter it prefers swampy pastures, flooded fields, marshes and lakes.

**NESTING** Lays 4 creamy eggs on a mound of vegetation. Chicks are active as soon as they hatch and are ready to migrate with their parents.

**RANGE** Migrates from Siberia in October to the Baltic region, northern Europe and Britain.

# BARNACLE GOOSE
## (BRANTA LEUCOPSIS)

The barnacle goose is a small black and white goose which is a winter visitor, seen from October to March. It has a black head with a white face and cheeks and a black bill, which distinguishes it from other geese. Its neck and chest are black and it has sharply contrasting white underparts with pale grey bars. Its dark grey upper parts are blue-grey barred. It has a white rump and a short black tail. Barnacle geese fly in close packs and long lines, and are very noisy and gregarious. Length: 59-69cm.

**VOICE** Flock can sound like a pack of yapping dogs. Makes a loud double note, which can be high pitched.

**HABITAT** On hilltops and slopes, near to coastal grasslands or rivers with plenty of nearby vegetation.

**NESTING** A hollow nest lined with down and laid on a cliff edge or rocky outcrop contains 3-6 grey eggs. Breeds in colonies.

**RANGE** Breeds in Greenland, Svalbard and Novaya Zemlya, wintering in north-western Britain, Ireland and northern Europe.

# BRENT GOOSE
## (BRANTA BERNICLA)

A small goose, almost the same size as a mallard duck. The Brent goose has a small head and a short neck, both of which are black, as is its breast and bill. Its throat is marked with a white collar, the size of which can vary according to the age of the bird; the collar is completely lacking in juveniles. Its back is dark grey and the light-bellied variety shows a marked contrast with the dark breast, whereas the dark-bellied type does not. It has a white rump. Noisy and gregarious, it is often seen in large flocks along the coast. Length: 56-61cm.

**Voice** Babbling calls and growling.
**Habitat** Breeds on Arctic tundra near to the sea, winters at shallow coasts, estuaries and coastal farmland.
**Nesting** 3-5 creamy eggs laid in a scrape near to water.
**Range** As far north as possible on Arctic coasts, wintering in northern Europe and nesting in Arctic Russia and Siberia.

# CANADA GOOSE (BRANTA CANADENSIS)

**VOICE** In flight a loud, double-note call with rise in second syllable.

**HABITAT** Found in large groups at freshwater sites and neighbouring fields and parkland.

**NESTING** Up to 5 eggs laid in a down-lined nest on short vegetation near freshwater.

**RANGE** Introduced from North America, now found in the British Isles, the Low Countries and Scandinavia, mostly as a permanent resident.

The canada goose is the largest of all geese found in Europe, with a long neck and erect stance giving it a swan-like silhouette. It has a black head, neck and bill with a distinctive white throat patch and white cheeks. Its large brown body is darker above and paler below, and its brown wings, body and chest mark it out from Brent and barnacle geese. It has white patches under its stern and black legs, and dark brown, almost black, tail feathers. The juvenile's markings are less distinct. Canada geese prefer to flock in large groups outside the breeding season and fly in regular lines or chevrons. Length: 90-100cm.

# (ANSER ANSER) GREYLAG GOOSE

Largest of the 'grey' geese, the greylag is the only one that breeds in Britain although many others migrate from Iceland in winter. It has grey-brown plumage which is barred in black on its back with a few spots on its belly. Its underparts are slightly lighter and it has a white stern. Its head and neck are grey brown, and it has wavy feather ridges on its neck. When flying, the dark flight feathers contrast with the blue-grey forewing. Its legs are pink and, in the British variety, the bill is bright orange without black markings. Eastern European greylags have pink bills. Length: 75-90cm.

**VOICE** Domestic birds gabble. Noisy calling in flocks.

**HABITAT** Lowland areas, suburban parks, lakes, marshes and estuaries; low-lying grassy fields.

**NESTING** 4-6 creamy eggs in a down-lined scrape.

**RANGE** Iceland, Scandinavia and Scotland down into more southern areas. Some migrate to Mediterranean.

# PINK-FOOTED GOOSE (ANSER BRACHYRHYNCHUS)

**Voice** Highly pitched and musical 'wink wink'.

**Habitat** Prefers farmland, moors and marshes for feeding; roosts on lakes, estuaries, rivers and mudflats.

**Nesting** Lays 4-6 creamy eggs in a hollow scrape on isolated islands and by rivers.

**Range** Breeds in Arctic circle, winters in northern Europe, particularly eastern England, France and the southern shores of the North Sea.

The pink-footed goose is a medium-sized, compact goose with a short neck and a relatively small bill. It has a dark brown head and neck, contrasting with its light pinkish-grey body and wings. Its back feathers have pale edges and its belly is also delicately barred. It has a white stripe on its body below its wings and a white rump. Its legs are pink. When flying, its pale grey wings are edged with darker grey flight feathers. A sociable bird, huge flocks of pink-footed geese fly in line formation at dusk to return to their roosting site after a day spent feeding. Length: 61-77cm.

# (ANSER ALBIFRONS) WHITE-FRONTED GOOSE

Two subspecies of white-fronted geese arrive in Britain during the winter, one from Greenland, the other from Russia. It is a medium-sized, grey goose with a long neck and a stocky chest. The western goose is slightly larger with darker plumage and an orange bill; the one arriving from the east has a pink bill. Both have grey-brown plumage which is lighter grey on the underparts. The upper parts are marked with faint pale lines, the neck, chest and belly are barred with black. Both have the characteristic white mark on the forehead and around the beak, which is absent in juveniles.
Length: 60-77cm.

**Voice** High-pitched cackling and yelping.
**Habitat** Breed on arctic tundra. When in Britain prefers wet grassland, bogs, estuaries and occasionally saltmarshes.
**Nesting** Lays 4-6 creamy eggs in a shallow scrape.
**Range** Winters across Europe, migrating from Arctic breeding grounds. In Britain, western birds prefer Ireland, while eastern birds visit south-eastern England.

# SHELDUCK (TADORNA TADORNA)

**VOICE** A range of whistles and growls. Females with a brood make a quick, nasal quack.

**HABITAT** Coastal, especially open mud and sand flats in estuaries and around the shoreline.

**NESTING** Large broods of up to 15 white eggs laid in down-lined burrows.

**RANGE** Across Europe from Ireland to Siberia. Common around the coast of the British Isles.

A large, goose-like duck. The shelduck appears to be black and white from a distance and in poor light, but its head and upper neck are actually a shiny dark green. Its body is predominantly white with a broad orange band on its chest and rear. It has black markings and a green patch on its wings, although they are mainly white. Its legs are a deep pink and its bill red, with a large knob found only in males. Juveniles are similar but they lack the chest band. In flight, its wing beat is slower than that of most ducks. Length 55-65cm.

# (ANAS STREPERA) GADWALL

Smaller than the mallard, the gadwall is a common grey dabbling duck. The male has grey plumage, delicately marked with white bars and speckles, with a bold black rear end. It has a white area on its side that shows up more clearly as a white wing patch when the bird is in flight. Its bill is black. The female is a mottled brown with a paler belly. She has orange streaks on the sides of her bill, and she too has a white wing patch which is visible at rest. Length: 46-56cm.

**VOICE** Quacking and croaking.
**HABITAT** Gravel pits, reservoirs, slow-flowing rivers and estuaries.
**NESTING** Lays 8-12 creamy eggs in a ground nest covered with thick vegetation.
**RANGE** Breeds across Europe from Iceland to Russia. Many winter south as far as the Mediterranean and Africa, with large numbers arriving in Britain.

# TEAL
## (ANAS CRECCA)

The teal is the smallest dabbling duck in Britain. The male teal has a chestnut head with yellow-bordered green eye patches. His body is grey, with spotted chest and grey flanks; a horizontal white stripe is another marked feature. The tail is black and edged with yellow and he has a distinctive yellow patch at the rear. The female is mottled brown instead of grey, with a brown-spotted underside. Both sexes have a bright green wing patch and white wing bars, which are particularly evident in flight. They both have dark grey bills. Teal fly in dense flocks, flying quickly and low. Length: 34-38cm.

**VOICE** Males make a whistling sound, females quack.

**HABITAT** Marshes, lakes, estuaries, shorelines. Wetlands offering cover and shallow water.

**NESTING** 8-12 creamy eggs laid in a nest on the ground in thick cover adjacent to shallow water.

**RANGE** Widespread across northern Europe and Eurasia. Some birds winter as far south as Africa.

# WIGEON (ANAS PENELOPE)

**VOICE** Male has a loud, high-pitched whistle, female a low growl.

**HABITAT** Shallow lakes, pools and marshes in the summer months, wintering on estuaries and around the shoreline.

**NESTING** 8-12 creamy-white eggs in a down and vegetation-lined nest concealed by more vegetation.

**RANGE** Breeds across northern Europe from Iceland to Russia, wintering around the coast of western Europe and the Mediterranean.

The wigeon is a rare breeder in the UK but a regular winter visitor. The male is predominantly grey, with a rusty, chestnut-coloured head and a yellow crown. Its upper parts are finely marked and its breast is pinkish. In flight it has a distinctive white forewing and a belly with a black stern. Both males and females have a small dark bill, a rounded head and a pointed tail, but females are a reddish-brown colour instead of grey. Wigeons are usually seen in large groups resting on the sea or grazing near fresh water, sometimes in the company of Brent geese. Length: 40-50 cm.

# (ANAS ACUTA) PINTAIL

The pintail is slightly larger than the mallard although more slender, with a small head and an elegant long neck. The male has a deep brown head and neck, with a white stripe extending up the side of the head from its white breast. Its body is a delicately marked blue-grey, with paler underparts. The rear end is creamy yellow, with the long, pointed, black tail often held slightly upwards. The female is typically brown, but shares the slender shape and long tail of her mate. In flight, the pintail has a curved back, with the extended neck and head held slightly downward, the wings pointed and the tail tapering. Length: 51-66cm.

**VOICE** Male has a drawn-out call, female quacks.

**HABITAT** Coastal marshes, estuaries, flooded grassland and lakes in winter.

**NESTING** Feather-lined hollows near to water contain 7-9 pale yellow-green eggs.

**RANGE** From Iceland, across Britain towards Bering Sea. Migrates to southern Europe and Africa.

# MALLARD
## (ANAS PLATYRHYNCHOS)

A large and heavy-looking bird, the mallard is perhaps the best-known duck, with both breeding birds and migrants resident in the UK. The male has a bright and glossy green head and a long, broad yellow bill. Its head is separated from its purple-brown breast by a white ring. Its body is long and the plumage is silvery grey, with a black rear and a black and white tail which curls upwards. The female is mainly brown and buff, with an orange bill and orange legs and feet. Both sexes have a blue wing patch with a white border. The female's colouring provides camouflage while she sits on the nest. Length: 50-65cm.

**VOICE** Male is quiet, female quacks.
**HABITAT** Large lakes, ponds, rivers, marshes and urban areas. Flocks can be seen on large lakes and the sea.
**NESTING** 10-12 pale green eggs in a feather and leaf-lined hollow, under cover and near to shallow water.
**RANGE** Widespread across Europe, Asia, North Africa and North America.

# MANDARIN (AIX GALERICULATA)

**VOICE** Usually silent.

**HABITAT** Lakes and slow-flowing rivers with vegetation. Requires tree hollows for nesting.

**NESTING** Nests in tree holes.

**RANGE** Native to east Asia. Found throughout south-eastern England and Norfolk.

Introduced to the UK from China, the mandarin duck has become an official resident in Britain and Ireland although most are to be found in the eastern corner of England. A highly ornate bird, the male mandarin has exotic plumage on its head and neck. Its cheeks are white and a broad black band extends from its short orange bill over the crown to the nape of the neck. It has long, orange feathers on the side of its face and orange 'sails' on its back. Its breast and back are black, its belly white and its side is muted orange. The female is less ornate, with a grey head, brown back and spotted grey breast and flanks. Length approx: 45cm.

# (ANAS QUERQUEDULA) GARGANEY

A slender duck, the garganey is smaller than a mallard and larger than a teal. It arrives in Britain during the summer, spending its winter in Africa. It is scarce as a result of extensive hunting in its winter home and along its migration route. The male is mottled brown with a broad white streak from the eye to the nape of the neck. It has a brown breast and a contrasting white belly. Its sides are grey with delicate stripes. Its long, drooping wing feathers are black and white and its forewing is blue-grey. When flying, both the male and the female show a green wing patch. The female is mottled brown with a striped head pattern. Length: 37-41cm.

**VOICE** Male rattles and burps, female quacks.
**HABITAT** Shallow, vegetated lakes; pools, marshes and flooded grasslands.
**NESTING** 8-11 creamy eggs in a hollow lined with plant material and down.
**RANGE** Winters in tropical Africa, breeds across Europe.

# SHOVELER
## (ANAS CLYPEATA)

The shoveler is a squat and short-necked duck with a very long, broad bill which is used for feeding. It sweeps its head from side to side, moving water through this specially adapted bill, filtering out its food. The shoveler's body tilts slightly forwards on the water, with the bill pointing downwards. The male has a dark green head, contrasting white breast and chestnut-coloured flanks. Its upper body is mainly black with some white stripes. When flying it shows patches of blue and green on its wings. The females are speckled brown, like the female mallard, but their distinctive bills mark them out. Like the male, the female shows green and blue patches on her forewing. Length: 44-52cm.

**VOICE** Male is generally quiet, female quacks.
**HABITAT** Reed-edged lakes and ponds, shallow water, prefers freshwater.
**NESTING** 8-12 olive eggs in a down-lined hollow adjacent to water.
**RANGE** Iceland, northern Europe, Scandinavia, across to Russia. In winter, some birds migrate to Africa.

# EIDER (SOMARTERIA MOLLISSIMA)

**Voice** Male croons and coos.
**Habitat** Rocky coasts, estuaries and offshore islands. Often found breeding in gull and tern colonies for protection.
**Nesting** 4-6 olive eggs in a hollow lined with down.
**Range** Prefers northern coasts of Europe for breeding.

The eider is a large, chunky sea duck. The male has white upper parts and black below. It has a black belly, rump and tail, and black flight feathers. The rest of its plumage is white except for its black crown. Its white breast is often tinged with pink and the nape of the neck is pale green. Juvenile males are more mottled and patchy. The female is brown with black barring. It has a triangular head with a flat forehead forming a continuous line with the wedge-shaped bill. It flies low and fast, in single file.
Length: 50-70cm.

# (MELANITTA NIGRA) COMMON SCOTER

The common scoter is the only British all-black duck, its one spot of colour being a yellow ridge on its bill which can only be seen at close range. The bill is topped by a black knob. The female is dark brown with pale brown cheeks and brownish-white underparts. A winter visitor, the common scoter can often be seen bobbing in large rafts on the waves in the company of other sea ducks. It dives in shallow water in search of molluscs and flies along the coast in straggly lines. Length: 44-54cm.

**VOICE** Whistles and hoots.
**HABITAT** Coasts and offshore islands, estuaries and sandy coasts. Breeds near lochs or on islands in lochs.
**NESTING** 6-9 creamy eggs in a feather-lined hollow under vegetation.
**RANGE** Iceland, northern Europe across to Bering Sea.

# GOLDENEYE (BUCEPHALA CLANGULA)

**Voice** Usually silent; male makes a nasal sound during courtship.

**Habitat** Inland lakes, large rivers, bays and estuaries. During breeding needs to be near trees for nesting.

**Nesting** Lays 6-11 turquoise eggs in a tree hole lined with feathers.

**Range** Breeds in Scandinavia, Iceland and northern Europe, winters further south towards Britain and Ireland.

A medium-sized, slightly chunky duck. The goldeneye has a large, domed head with a short neck. The male has a dark green head and a bright yellow eye. It has a distinctive white patch on its cheek at the base of the black bill. Its plumage is a striking combination of black and white, with black wings, back and tail and white breast and belly. In flight it shows large white patches on its wings. The female is a mottled grey, with a dark brown head and neck. Like the male the female has black wings, but she has a white square patch as opposed to the male's white stripes. Both have orange legs.
Length: 42-50cm.

# (AYTHYA FERINA) POCHARD

A compact and stocky duck, the pochard is smaller than a mallard with an unmistakable chestnut-coloured head. Its dome-shaped head is large, with a high forehead. Only the male has a red head and neck; the female is mottled brown and grey. The male has a black breast and rump and delicately marked grey back and flanks. In flight, his grey wings show a paler grey wing bar. Both sexes have a dark bill with a grey-blue band across it. An expert diver, the pochard has large webbed feet, making it clumsy on land. Length: 42-49cm.

**VOICE** Usually silent. Male whistles softly during courtship.

**HABITAT** Lakes, reservoirs, gravel pits, marshes and estuaries.

**NESTING** Lays 6-11 pale green eggs in a nest on or in water.

**RANGE** Across northern Europe and Eurasia; some birds migrate south towards Africa.

# RUDDY DUCK (OXYURA JAMAICENSIS)

**VOICE** Mostly silent.

**HABITAT** Open freshwater locations, breeds on small lakes, reservoirs and wetlands with plenty of nearby vegetation.

**NESTING** 6-10 white eggs in a down-lined nest amongst water vegetation.

**RANGE** Mainly American continent. Can be found in Midlands, northern England, southern Scotland and North Wales. Extending to France.

The ruddy duck is a small, slightly dumpy freshwater duck. The male has a black head and neck with white cheeks below the eye. Its body has bright chestnut plumage and a black rump. Its black tail is stiff and often cocked to point upwards. The female is similar to the male, but with greyer body plumage and a less-pronounced cheek patch. Both sexes have a broad, bright blue bill. The ruddy duck rarely leaves the water, either to walk or fly. It can submerge without diving. Imported into Britain from North America, it is now partially responsible for the scarcity of the white-headed duck. Length: 35-43cm.

# (AYTHYA FULIGULA) TUFTED DUCK

A medium-sized diving duck which can be seen all year round throughout the UK. The tufted duck is mainly black with white underparts and a white stripe across the back of the wing which is particularly conspicuous in flight. Its marking feature is a drooping black crest or tuft on its head. Although the head looks black, at close range a purple sheen can be detected. The female is dark brown and lacks the long tuft of the male, showing instead a short crest. Both sexes have a bright yellow eye and a narrow pale band on the base of the blue-grey bill.
Length: 40-47cm.

**VOICE** Male whistles, female growls although they are mostly silent.
**HABITAT** Prefers inland lakes and larger bodies of water, including slow-flowing rivers. Urban areas.
**NESTING** 5-12 pale green eggs in a feather-lined nest near water.
**RANGE** Iceland and northern Europe. Some migrate as far south as North Africa.

# GOOSANDER (MERGUS MERGANSER)

**Voice** Mostly silent.
**Habitat** Upland rivers and streams, some upland lakes and lochs. Often forms large flocks.
**Nesting** Lays 7-14 yellowish eggs in a down-lined nest in tree trunks or ground hollows.
**Range** Breeds in Iceland, northern Europe and Scandinavia, across to Bering Sea. Winters in northern Europe.

A large and elegant sawbill duck, the goosander has a long red bill with a hooked tip and serrated edge which is used for catching fish. The male has a dark green head and its body is mostly pure white, with the occasional pink blush on its breast. Its back is black. Its red bill is matched with red eyes and red legs and feet. The female has a brown head and neck, and mostly grey plumage on her body. She also has a short, drooping crest on her head and a white patch on her chin, both of which mark her out. Goosanders are disliked by salmon and trout fishermen because of their diet of fish.
Length: 58-66cm.

# (MERGUS SERRATOR) RED-BREASTED MERGANSER

The red-breasted merganser is a smaller sawbill duck than its relative the goosander. Both sexes have a distinctive and ragged double crest at the back of the head and a long, red bill. The male has a dark black-green head with a sharply contrasting white collar. It has a chestnut-red, speckled breast band which is separated from the body by a broad black band with white patches. The male's body is mostly light grey, with black lines on the wings. The female has a chestnut-red head and darker crest and her body is brownish-grey and mottled. The female can be distinguished by white wing patches. Length: 52-58cm.

**Voice** Croaking call. Usually silent.
**Habitat** Freshwater lakes, slow rivers and sheltered estuaries. Often found wintering in coastal areas.
**Nesting** 7-12 creamy green eggs in a hollow lined with down and plant material. Nests near to water.
**Range** Iceland, northern Europe across to Bering Sea. Winters south, some reaching Mediterranean.

# RED KITE
## (MILVUS MILVUS)

The red kite is a slender, long-winged bird of prey, with an unmistakable deeply forked tail. Its upper body is a rich brown and its chest, belly and rump are chestnut red, as is its long tail. It has a small, pale grey head, yellow feet and a small, yellow, black-tipped bill. At rest, its wings are brown, showing some black and white; in flight, they are long, angular and show a white patch on the underside with black tips and a pale brown wing bar. The red kite soars in the air effortlessly, lending its name to the child's toy. It uses its long and distinctively forked tail to steer by twisting it constantly. Length: 56-64cm; wingspan: 145-165cm.

**VOICE** Mewing and whistling.
**HABITAT** Deciduous woodland, close to agricultural land and grassland.
**NESTING** 2-4 white-spotted eggs in a nest built in a tree.
**RANGE** From north Africa up into southern and central Europe. More common in Wales, but reintroduced into England and Scotland.

# MARSH HARRIER (CIRCUS AERUGINOSUS)

**VOICE** Mostly silent.

**HABITAT** Fens, swamps and marshland with large reed beds. Seen in fields near wetlands.

**NESTING** Around 5 pale blue eggs laid in a large nest built from twigs, concealed in reed bed.

**RANGE** Across Eurasia, from Spain to Japan. Resident in Kent and a summer visitor to other parts of the UK.

The marsh harrier is larger and more heavily built than the other harriers. It has long, narrow wings, which are broader than those of its relatives. Males have a brown body which is darker on the back. The head is a lighter, buff colour and its grey tail is long with a square end. Its flight feathers are black and it has a grey band on the upper wings. Females have predominantly brown bodies with a cream crown, throat and shoulders, and a distinctive black mark across the eye. Juveniles tend to resemble the female, being more brown than grey. The marsh harrier's flight is low with steady wing beats and long glides. When soaring they have 'v'-shaped wings. Length: 50-55cm; wingspan: 110-125cm.

# (CIRCUS CYANEUS) HEN HARRIER

A slimmer harrier, with a long body, wings and tail. The male hen harrier is silver-grey above with a paler belly. It has striking black wing tips and a black edge to its wings that is mostly seen in flight. It also has a conspicuous white rump. Females and juveniles have dark brown upper parts and paler brown underparts which are streaked with dark grey. The female also has a pale collar. Gregarious out of the breeding season, they roost collectively in winter. Their flight is low with long glides and the wings are held in a shallow 'v'. Length: 40-50cm; wingspan: 100-120cm.

**VOICE** Usually silent.

**HABITAT** Prefers open moorland with heather and mixed vegetation. Can also be found on coastal marshes, fenland and farmland.

**NESTING** Lays 4-6 blue eggs in a ground nest.

**RANGE** Across northern Europe, including northern Spain, through Scandinavia to Bering Sea. Some migrate further south.

# SPARROWHAWK
## (ACCIPITER NISUS)

The sparrowhawk is a common and widespread bird of prey. The male is relatively small, with short, rounded wings and a long, narrow, square-ended tail. The female is substantially larger. Both sexes have grey upper parts; however the male is slate grey, the female somewhat browner. The male has white underparts with closely barred orange markings. He also has reddish cheeks with a dark grey crown and nape. The male's throat is white. The female also has white underparts but with brown bars. She has a long, pale eye stripe. Both sexes have dark barring on their long tails. The broad, rounded wings and long tail are designed to enable swift flight through trees in search of prey. Length: 28-38cm; wingspan: 60-75cm.

**VOICE** A rapid 'kek kek kek'.
**HABITAT** Prefers conifer woodland for nesting, but found in other arboreal areas. Some have moved into urban areas and are occasional garden visitors.
**NESTING** 4-5 brown and blue eggs are laid in a tree nest.
**RANGE** Found across Europe with some migrating south towards Africa.

# GOSHAWK
## (ACCIPITER GENTILIS)

Although much larger than its cousin the sparrowhawk, the goshawk has relatively short, rounded wings and a slightly shorter tail. The female is larger than the male. The male is grey-brown on the back, with pale, almost white plumage on its underparts which are marked with brown bars. It has a white streak 'eyebrow' and a dark patch behind its yellow eye, all making it look fierce. Its tail has several broad dark bands. The female has browner plumage. During flight, it can be seen to 'fluff up' its white undertail feathers in display.
Length: 48-59cm;
wingspan: 100-115cm.

**VOICE** Insistent chattering and screams.
**HABITAT** Mature woods and forests, particularly coniferous. Hunts in open countryside and glades.
**NESTING** 2-4 bluish eggs are laid in a large tree nest.
**RANGE** Breeds throughout Europe.

# BUZZARD
## (BUTEO BUTEO)

The most common bird of prey in the UK, the buzzard is medium in size with a short, thick neck, short tail and a large, rounded head. Its plumage can vary, ranging from almost white to very dark brown. In general, its wings and back are barred brown and its underparts are paler with dark bars. All have dark wing tips and unbarred tails. In darker birds, a broad and pale chest band is visible. Its wings are broad and rounded and it holds them in a shallow 'v' when it soars in the air. Its short bill is black and its legs yellow. Buzzards can often be seen perched on fence posts and dead branches. Length: 51-56cm; wingspan: 115-125cm.

**VOICE** A loud mewing.
**HABITAT** Prefers trees and crags when breeding and open fields for feeding.
**NESTING** Lays 3-4 red-blotched eggs in a bulky nest off the ground. Incubated by the female.
**RANGE** Across Europe with some migrating in northern Africa.

# ROUGH-LEGGED BUZZARD (BUTEO LAGOPUS)

**VOICE** Usually silent.

**HABITAT** Barren hills, moorlands, fields and coastal sites close to open woodland for roosting.

**NESTING** Lays 2-4 eggs which are white with red spots in a tree nest or on a cliff edge.

**RANGE** Breeds in Scandinavia, winters in Britain and eastern central Europe.

The rough-legged buzzard is larger than the buzzard, with longer wings and a long tail. The female is slightly larger than the male. It has grey-brown upper parts with a paler grey head. Its pale breast is streaked with brown and it has a contrasting black belly. Its tail is white with dark banding and a broad terminal band. Its underwings are pale with dark edging and wing tips, and a black 'elbow' patch. The juvenile has more defined markings than the adult. When soaring it holds its wings in a shallow 'v' and often flaps them while hovering. Length: 50-60cm; wingspan: 125-145cm.

# (PERNIS APIVORUS) HONEY BUZZARD

The honey buzzard passes over Britain when migrating, although some do breed in the UK. It is a large bird of prey, with a proportionally long tail and a small, slender head. The typical adult has dark brown upper parts and much paler underparts which are heavily barred. Its head is grey, often with a more brownish crown. Its tail has distinctive dark bars and a black tip and is slightly round at the end. In flight, its barred underwings show a dark 'elbow' patch. Unlike other buzzards, the honey buzzard soars on flat wings. Length: 50-58cm; wingspan: 135-160cm.

**VOICE** Usually silent.

**HABITAT** Prefers mature, deciduous woodland, but can be found in conifer forests. Spends winters in African forests.

**NESTING** Lays 1-3 buff eggs spotted with brown in a high tree nest.

**RANGE** Summer visitor across central and eastern Europe; migrates to tropical Africa.

# GOLDEN EAGLE
## (AQUILA CHRYSAETOS)

A large eagle with a broad wingspan. The golden eagle is one of the largest birds found in the UK. Its body is mainly dark brown, with some white patches seen on the wings; the crown and short neck are a golden brown, earning it its name. In flight it can look quite dark. Its wings are long and relatively narrow and its tail is long and gently rounded. It has a grey, hooked bill, grey legs and taloned feet. Juvenile birds have white patches on the wings and a white tail with a black band. Golden eagles soar when they fly and can hold their wings in a shallow 'v'.
Length: 76-90cm;
wingspan: 190-225cm.

**VOICE** Yelping calls.
**HABITAT** Prefers high mountainous regions with open areas for hunting. Golden eagles are very territorial, with nesting sites often being used for generations.
**NESTING** Lays 1-2 white, blotchy eggs in a nest on a cliff edge.
**RANGE** Is wide-ranging; can be found across mountainous regions in Europe. In Britain is most commonly found in the Scottish Highlands.

The golden eagle has an
enormous wingspan of up
to 225 centimetres.

# OSPREY
## (PANDION HALIAETUS)

The osprey is a large, heavy raptor with long, angled wings and a small head and bill. Its back and wings are dark brown and its chest, belly and underwings are white and slightly mottled. It has a white crown and throat, and a distinctive dark stripe from its eye to the neck. It has darkly barred flight feathers and a barred tail, and a black patch on the 'wrists' of its wings which is most obvious when in flight. It also has a brown band across its breast which tends to be darker in the female. Ospreys are the only British birds of prey to dive into water in order to catch fish. They are often mistaken for large gulls due to their narrow, bowed wings and pale colouring. Length: 51-59cm; wingspan: 145-160cm.

**VOICE** A shrill, repeated whistle.
**HABITAT** Favours areas near to water, usually pine forests close to lakes and rivers.
**NESTING** Eggs are yellow with red spots; 3 are laid in a nest in a tree or on a cliff.
**RANGE** Found on every continent. Visits northern and eastern Europe from Africa during the summer.

# KESTREL
## (FALCO TINNUNCULUS)

The kestrel is Britain's commonest and most familiar falcon. It is relatively small with long, pointed wings and a long tail. The male's back and wings are a light red-brown marked with dark spots. Its head and neck are a blue-grey with a white throat and a narrow black moustache, while its underparts are pale and buffy with black spots. Its long tail is grey, barred in black, with a dark band across the end. The female has a brown head and brown upper parts marked with black spots. Kestrels are a common sight on motorway verges, where they can be seen hovering as they hunt for prey. Length: 33-35cm; wingspan: 65-80cm.

**VOICE** High-pitched 'kee kee'.
**HABITAT** Open countryside, towns and cities, coast – anywhere a suitable nesting site can be found. Tends to avoid dense forests and mountainous areas. Upland birds will often move to warmer areas in winter.
**NESTING** Lays white eggs in a hole or on a ledge, cliff edge, tree or even a building.
**RANGE** Found across Europe, though not as far north as Iceland.

# MERLIN (FALCO COLUMBARIUS)

**VOICE** High-pitched, rapid chatter.
**HABITAT** Breeds in open moorland, spends winters in a variety of locations, from coastal marshes to inland agricultural areas.
**NESTING** 4-5 brown-spotted eggs are laid in a ground hollow and incubated by the female.
**RANGE** Mainly northern Europe, Scandinavia and Iceland across to Bering Sea.

Britain's smallest bird of prey, the merlin has a relatively long tail and short, pointed wings. It has a sturdy breast. The male is blue-grey above with buffy underparts that are streaked with brown and black. The female is larger than the male and her plumage is brown rather than grey. Both sexes have a dark bar across the end of the tail and neither of them has the moustache common to most other falcons. The merlin flies low over the ground and its small size enables it to hover. Its flight often resembles that of a thrush; it dashes and bounces in pursuit of its prey. Length:25-33cm; wingspan: 60-65cm.

# (FALCO SUBBUTEO) HOBBY

The hobby is a small and slender falcon with long, narrow, sickle-shaped wings and a relatively short tail. Its upper parts are slate grey, and its breast, belly and underwings are white, heavily marked with black streaks. Its cheeks and throat are white and it has a narrow and pointed black moustache. It has red plumage on its thighs and under its tail. Juveniles are browner above with a pinkish colour below. The hobby catches its prey in flight and as a result is a fast flier capable of impressive, high-speed acrobatics. Length: 35-40cm; wingspan: 70-85cm.

**VOICE** Rapid, high-pitched 'kew kew'.
**HABITAT** Prefers trees in farmland and woodland for breeding; heathland and open countryside for feeding.
**NESTING** Lays 2-3 yellow and brown eggs in an abandoned tree nest.
**RANGE** Winters in Asia and Africa, visits most of temperate Europe during the summer. More common in central and southern parts of Britain.

# PEREGRINE
## (FALCO PEREGRINUS)

A small but powerful raptor, the peregrine has narrow, pointed wings and a short tail. Its upper parts are dark blue-grey, the underparts are white with striking black bars. Its flight feathers are white with grey bars. Its white cheek bears a prominent black moustache and its crown is almost black. Peregrines soar and perform acrobatics in flight, and they strike at their prey by diving at great speed. Its diet of pigeon brought about a cataclysmic cull during WWII to prevent the thwarting of messenger pigeons. At one time the peregrine faced possible extinction, due to habitat pollution and the loss of its young to falconry; however the population is now on the increase. Length: 38-48cm; wingspan: 95-115cm.

**VOICE** Usually silent. Can make high-pitched calls when nesting.
**HABITAT** Mountains, coastal cliffs, offshore islands and even buildings. Prefers estuaries, marshes and moorland in winter.
**NESTING** Breeds mainly on cliff faces, laying 3-4 red-speckled eggs which are incubated by the female for 28 days.
**RANGE** Is common throughout Europe, although the Scandinavian and eastern birds migrate southwards during the winter with some venturing as far as Africa.

# RED GROUSE (LAGOPUS LAGOPUS SCOTICUS)

**VOICE** Crowing and cackling; makes characteristic 'go back, go back' call.

**HABITAT** Prefers heather moorlands, bogs and farmland, coastal heaths and scrubland.

**NESTING** Lays 6-11 creamy eggs in a ground hollow under cover.

**RANGE** Breeds in Britain and Ireland across to Scandinavia and north Russia. Tends not to migrate.

The red grouse is a plump, medium-sized game bird with a short tail and short wings. The male has red-brown, delicately striped plumage and slightly darker-coloured wings and tail which are most obvious when in flight. He also has a small red wattle over his eye. The female is less red but otherwise very similar to the male. Her marbled plumage provides good camouflage as she sits on the nest. Both sexes have legs and feet covered in pale feathers. Its bill is short and slightly hooked. It flies with rapid wing beats alternating with long glides. Length: 37-42cm.

# (TETRAO TETRIX) BLACK GROUSE

The male black grouse is slightly larger than the grey-brown female and at a distance may appear to be totally black. At close range, the plumage can be seen to be blue-black with a bright red wattle above the eye and a white shoulder patch. It has a white stripe across its wing which is particularly striking during flight. Its tail is forked or lyre-shaped and when fanned out reveals the distinctive white rump feathers that are used for courtship displays. Males gather together in 'leks' to attract mates, leaping, displaying, singing and fighting. The female can be identified by her slightly notched tail and her pale wing bar. Length: 40-55cm.

**VOICE** Sneezing and bubbling.
**HABITAT** Upland moors, farmland and woodland.
**NESTING** Lays 6-10 creamy eggs spotted with brown on the ground under cover.
**RANGE** Northern and eastern Europe across to Siberia and Asia.

# PTARMIGAN
(LAGOPUS MUTUS)

Slightly smaller than the red grouse, the ptarmigan prefers mountainous northern regions such as the Scottish Highlands. In summer, the male has dark grey-brown plumage on its upper parts with white wings and belly. The female has brown plumage on her back, marked with black bars and spots. Both sexes begin to moult during the autumn, becoming mottled in brown, grey and white. By winter they have turned completely white except for their black tails. The male also retains a black eye patch and a red comb above the eye. Their colouring acts as effective camouflage, helping them to blend in with the snow during winter and the boulders during summer. Length: 33-38cm.

**VOICE** Croaking and crowing.
**HABITAT** High mountains, rarely seen below 700m.
**NESTING** 5-10 creamy eggs are laid on the ground amongst boulders or vegetation.
**RANGE** Northern mountainous regions such as Scotland, Iceland, north-eastern Russia and Scandinavia. Can be found in the Pyrenees and the Alps.

# CAPERCAILLIE (TETRAO UROGALLUS)

**VOICE** Clicks and pops.
**HABITAT** Mature pine forests with plenty of ground vegetation.
**NESTING** Lays 5-8 yellow and brown eggs in a nest covered with ground vegetation.
**RANGE** Scotland, Scandinavia and some parts of central Europe, wherever suitable pine forests can be found.

An enormous grouse, the male capercaillie is much larger than the female. Its heavy build and broad, fanned tail mark it out from other game birds. The male appears to be all black, but at close range has a slate grey head, neck and back, and a black tail marked with delicate white bands. Its dark breast has a greenish tinge and its wings are slightly brown with a white patch on the shoulder. It has a long, thick neck, a small red wattle above its eye and a yellow bill. It fans its tail when displaying. The female is mottled grey-brown with dark bars on her back and white markings on the breast and belly. She has a red-brown breast and tail. Length: male: 82-90cm; female: 58-64cm.

# (ALECTORIS RUFA) RED-LEGGED PARTRIDGE

The red-legged partridge is a rotund bird, slightly larger than its grey cousin. The sexes are very similar. Its upper parts are blue-grey with a brown blush. Its flanks are distinctively barred with black, brown and white vertical stripes. Its cheeks and throat are white and it has a black mask and collar which breaks up into spots further down the throat and onto the breast. It has a bright red bill, eye ring and, as its name suggests, red legs. A reluctant flyer, it tends to run away from danger. When it does take to the air, its flight is low and its wings are bowed. Length: 32-34cm.

**Voice** A 'chuk chuk' call.
**Habitat** Open fields, sandy or scrubby country.
**Nesting** 10-16 yellow eggs with red and grey blotches are laid in a hollow on the ground.
**Range** South-western Europe, introduced to Britain.

# GREY PARTRIDGE (PERDIX PERDIX)

**Voice** Cackling calls.
**Habitat** Prefers short grass, stubble fields and hedgerows. Can be found on both agricultural land and moors and heaths.
**Nesting** Lays 9-20 olive-brown eggs in a covered shallow nest on ground.
**Range** Found across Europe, from the Atlantic coasts to Russia and Asia.

A smallish game bird, the grey partridge has a round body, short, rounded wings and a short tail. Its upper parts and tail are streaked with brown, buff and black and its chest and belly are a finely marked grey. It has chestnut barring on its flanks and a dark brown patch on its belly. Its face and throat are a distinctive orange colour and its tail has orange corners which appear as streaks when the bird is at rest. It flies fast, low and noisily but is primarily a ground dweller and not to be found in pear trees.
Length: 29-31cm.

# (COTURNIX COTURNIX) QUAIL

A small member of the partridge family, the quail has a dumpy little body and a very short tail. In flight it shows long, pointed wings. Its upper body is mainly brown, streaked and barred with black and white, and its breast and belly are a buffy pale brown. It has dark streaks on its flanks. Its head is small and brown with pale stripes down the centre and above the eye. The male has a black and white throat, the female a buff one. A shy bird, its plumage enables it to remain concealed in tall vegetation and it rarely flies. The quail is more usually heard than seen, with its distinctive, persistent call. Length: 15-18cm.

**VOICE** A repeated call of three notes – 'wick-wick-wick'.

**HABITAT** Prefers open spaces with tall vegetation such as agricultural pastures and grasslands.

**NESTING** Lays 7-12 pale yellow eggs with brown spots in a shallow, covered ground nest.

**RANGE** Spends the summer from central and eastern Europe, to Asia. Winters in northern Africa and the Sahara.

# PHEASANT
## (PHASIANUS COLCHICUS)

A large game bird with a
characteristic long tail, the
pheasant has a sturdy body and
short, rounded wings. The
colourful male is larger than
the mottled brown female.
Introduced from Asia for
sport, the plumage of males
can vary depending upon the
subspecies. In general the male
has a metallic blue-green head,
with short ear tufts and large
red eye wattles. Its body is a
golden brown with fine black
markings, and the tail is
chestnut with heavy black
bars. Some have a white collar
and others have paler brown
plumage on the body. The
female has a shorter tail than
the male, but it is still
relatively long.
Length: 53-59cm.

**Voice** Loud, far-carrying crowing.
**Habitat** Prefers woodland and
hedgerows for breeding, often
found in open fields. Many are
bred in captivity and released for
shooting.
**Nesting** Lays 7-15 olive eggs in a
shallow ground nest under cover.
**Range** Native to Asia, but
introduced throughout Europe.

# CORNCRAKE (CREX CREX)

**VOICE** Persistently repeated and harsh double-note call.

**HABITAT** Prefers tall grass and vegetation, often inhabits agricultural fields before they are harvested.

**NESTING** Lays 8-12 brown-blotched eggs in a grassy ground nest.

**RANGE** Visits central and eastern Europe during the summer, winters in south east Africa.

A secretive and shy bird, the corncrake does not live on water unlike other crakes and rails. It is slim and long-legged, with a short, stubby yellow bill. Its back and upper wings are a yellow-brown boldly marked with black. It has a grey-brown face, throat and chest. Its belly and flanks are marked with chestnut bars and it has bright chestnut wing patches that are particularly conspicuous in flight. It takes to the air reluctantly and when flying trails its long pink legs. Although difficult to see, the corncrake announces its presence with a loud, rasping call.
Length: 27-30cm.

# (RALLUS AQUATICUS) WATER RAIL

Larger than its crake relatives, the water rail is a slim marsh bird with long legs, a distinctive long red bill and short, rounded wings. Its upper parts are olive-brown, streaked with black markings. Its face, throat, breast and belly are slate grey and its flanks are striped with black and white. It often holds its tail cocked, revealing its white undertail feathers. Its narrow body allows it to move quickly and easily through its reed bed habitat. When it flies, its long pink legs and feet can be seen trailing behind.
Length: 23-28cm.

**VOICE** Squealing, grunting and purring.
**HABITAT** Prefers water with plenty of vegetation such as marshes, reed beds and ditches.
**NESTING** Lays 6-11 creamy, grey-spotted eggs in a covered ground nest.
**RANGE** Found throughout Europe, including Iceland and southern Scandinavia. Some birds migrate south as far as Africa.

# MOORHEN
## (GALLINULA CHLOROPUS)

The moorhen is a common and widespread water bird. It is medium in size, although smaller than the similar coot. From a distance the moorhen looks black, but in fact its back is a dark brown and its underparts are a deep blue-grey. It has a distinctive white stripe along its side and a patch of white plumage under its tail. Its bill is red with a yellow tip and it also has a red 'shield' at the top. Its long, sturdy legs are green with a red band next to the body. Juvenile moorhens are brown, with a greenish bill and shield. As it swims, the moorhen nods its head and jerks its highly held tail constantly. Length: 32-35cm.

**Voice** Loud quacking and clucking.
**Habitat** Freshwater lakes, rivers and ponds. Often found in urban areas.
**Nesting** 5-11 pale grey, brown-spotted eggs are laid in a ground nest near to water.
**Range** Widespread across Europe with the exception of northern Scandinavia.

# COOT
## (FULICA ATRA)

A slightly dumpy water bird, the coot is larger than its cousin the moorhen. It is black with dark, slate-grey plumage on its body and a pure black head and neck. Unlike the moorhen, the coot has no white markings on its body, but instead has a white bill and shield on its face. Its legs are green and its toes have lobed flaps of skin which act like webs when swimming. Juveniles are much paler, with grey plumage and an almost white throat and breast and no white shield. Coots nod their heads when swimming and dive expertly, bobbing back to the surface like corks. Length: 32-35cm.

**VOICE** A loud 'kuwk' sound.
**HABITAT** Shallow, fresh water with reed margins and vegetation. Often seen in urban lakes and ponds. Occasionally found on the coast in winter.
**NESTING** Lays 6-9 pale yellow, brown-spotted eggs in a large nest attached to bankside vegetation.
**RANGE** Resident to western Europe, a summer visitor elsewhere.

# AVOCET (RECURVIROSTRA AVOSETTA)

**VOICE** A short, fluting call.
**HABITAT** Shallow coastal waters, estuaries, saltmarshes and some freshwater marshes.
**NESTING** Lays 4 black and buff, blotchy eggs in a bare hollow, to be incubated by both parents.
**RANGE** Summer visitor to coastal areas in Europe, winters in Mediterranean and Africa.

Used by the RSPB as their symbol, the avocet is a large, yet slim and elegant, wader. It has mainly pure white plumage, with bold black markings on the wings and tail feathers. It has a black crown which covers the eye and continues along to the nape of the neck. Its black bill is very long and slim, and turns upwards at the end. The avocet can be seen sweeping its bill through the water in search of food. The very long legs are blue-grey. When flying, its long wings are pointed, showing black tips, and its legs trail behind. Length: 43cm.

# (HAEMATOPUS OSTRALEGUS) OYSTERCATCHER

A large black and white pied shore bird, the oystercatcher is distinctive with its long, deep orange bill and pink legs and feet. The black feathers extend over the neck and head, and in flight bold white wing bars can be seen. It has a white bar across the throat in winter, which is also present in juveniles. A sturdy, noisy bird, it can often be seen in flocks around the coast, flying low and circling over the water, the head and bill pointing downwards as it yelps excitedly. In flight it moves rather like a duck, with quick, shallow beats. Primarily feeds on molluscs and worms. Length approx: 43cm.

**Voice** Loud and shrill, with a trilling 'beek' sound.

**Habitat** Common on shores, islands and coastal meadows in both Britain and Ireland. Often inland during the summer.

**Nesting** Lays 3 black and yellow, blotchy eggs in a scrape, incubated by both parents.

**Range** Britain, northern Europe and Scandinavia all year round. Occasional visitor to Baltic region for breeding although eastern birds migrate westwards, wintering around North Sea.

# STONE CURLEW (BURHINUS OEDICNEMUS)

**Voice** Similar to that of a curlew, a shrill whistling call.

**Habitat** Prefers downlands and heaths for breeding; is often spotted on bare, stony ground with sparse vegetation.

**Nesting** Lays 2 brown-blotched eggs on the ground.

**Range** A summer visitor to Europe, occasionally seen in southern England. Migrates to Africa.

A big wading bird, the stone curlew has a large round head, a long tail and long wings. Its plumage is sandy coloured with dark brown streaks. It has a distinctive black and white stripe on its closed wing that becomes a bold wing bar when the bird is in flight; its flight feathers are a dark grey. Its large yellow eyes are enhanced by white 'brows'. It has long, thick, yellow legs and a relatively long neck, which give it height as it stretches to scan its environment. When it is disturbed it will lie flat to avoid detection. Rarely seen, but often recognized by its call.
Length: 41-43 cm.

# (VANELLUS VANELLUS) LAPWING

Once widespread, the lapwing is still a common sight in northern England and southern Scotland. From a distance it can appear simply black and white, but at close range it is more colourful. Its upper parts are dark grey, shot with an iridescent green, and it has chestnut plumage under its tail. It has a white neck and belly separated by a black breast band which spreads up onto the throat. The male sports a long, curving, black crest while the female is paler with a shorter crest. In flight, the lapwing has very rounded black and white wings. Length approx: 30cm.

**Voice** A loud 'pee wit' call.
**Habitat** Prefers farmland, particularly bare and ploughed fields for breeding. Can also be found on estuaries and wet grassland.
**Nesting** Lays 4 brown-blotched eggs in a well-hidden ground nest.
**Range** Found across Europe, moving westwards from colder climates during winter.

# RINGED PLOVER (CHARADRIUS HIATICULA)

**Voice** Low whistling and trilling.
**Habitat** Sandy and shingle beaches, coastal lagoons and some gravel pits.
**Nesting** 4 olive-grey eggs are laid in a hollow scrape amongst shingle.
**Range** Northern coasts of Europe including Scandinavia; many winter in Britain.

The ringed plover is a small, plump plover with short legs. It has a distinctive broad black band across its white breast, and black bars through its eye and across its crown. The back of its crown, its back, tail and upper wings are a sandy brown colour. Its underparts are white and it has an orange bill tipped with black, and orange legs. When flying it has long, pointed wings and it shows a broad white wing bar. In winter, and in younger birds, its darker plumage can become paler and less striking. The ringed plover can usually be seen running quickly then standing still for a few seconds before bowing to pick up food. Length: 18-20cm.

# (CHARADRIUS DUBIUS) LITTLE RINGED PLOVER

Smaller than the ringed plover with a few marked differences, the little ringed plover is the freshwater equivalent of its relative. It has a small round head with a brown crown and a black and white face, marked by a black eye stripe and crown stripe. Its brown back and wings are separated from the head and neck by a bold black collar. Its underparts are white. In flight its wings do not show a wing bar, unlike those of its relative. Its bill is black and it has an orange eye ring. Its legs are pale, a flesh colour rather than orange.
Length: approx 15cm.

**VOICE** A whistling song.
**HABITAT** Prefers shingle near to freshwater lakes, particularly gravel pits and reservoirs. Can be found near rivers with sandy edges.
**NESTING** 4 grey-brown eggs are laid in a scrape on sand or gravel.
**RANGE** Spends the summer months in Europe and winters in Asia and Africa.

# GOLDEN PLOVER (PLUVIALIS APRICARIA)

**VOICE** Melancholy whistling.
**HABITAT** Breeds in upland moorlands, pastures and bogs. Also found on bare and ploughed farmland.
**NESTING** Lays 3-4 buff, brown-spotted eggs in a scrape among grasses.
**RANGE** Summer visitor to northern Europe and Scandinavia, heads further south towards Mediterranean during winter.

The golden plover is a medium-sized and upright wader. During the breeding season, the males sport the bold markings that earn them their name, although in winter they can appear brown and less interesting. During summer, its dark upper parts are richly spotted with gold. The jet-black plumage on its throat and underparts is split by a white streak curving between the face and tail. Its cheeks are grey and its bill is black. In flight, the plumage under its wings is pale grey and it has a pale wing bar. Length: 25-28cm.

# (CALIDRIS CANUTUS) KNOT

A stocky wader, the knot has a short neck and legs and a relatively short bill. In winter its plumage is grey above and white below. It has a grey crown with a white stripe above the eye. Its throat and breast are white with delicate grey markings. Its wings are long and pointed, showing narrow white bars when flying. During the summer its chest, belly and face are red, with darker markings on its upper parts. Its bill is straight and dark and its legs are green. Knots flock in huge numbers, forming giant, twisting clouds.
Length: 25cm.

**Voice** A low 'nut nut' call.
**Habitat** Seashores and estuaries.
**Nesting** Lays 4 olive-streaked eggs in a shallow ground nest.
**Range** Winters in Arctic circle, particularly Greenland and Siberia. Spends summers in European coastal areas.

# SANDERLING (CALIDRIS ALBA)

**Voice** Makes a 'twick twick' sound in flight.

**Habitat** Found on sandy and rocky shores, and estuaries.

**Nesting** 4 olive-green eggs are laid in a hollow covered with vegetation.

**Range** Breeds on land in the Arctic circle, migrates south through Europe to Africa.

A small, plump and lively wader, the sanderling follows breaking waves in and out searching for food. It has pale grey upper parts and is white underneath. Most of its head appears white, although it has delicate grey markings on its crown. Its summer plumage is rarely seen in the UK as it is a migrant: its upper parts become russet brown with dark markings, and it has brown streaks on its white breast. It has a black shoulder patch, black legs and a short black bill. When flying it shows a bold white wing bar. Length: 20cm.

# (CALIDRIS ALPINA) DUNLIN

A common small wader. In summer, the dunlin has a reddish-brown, mottled crown, back and upper wings. It has a distinctive black patch on its white belly, white underparts and a white chest with black streaks. Its legs are sturdy and black. In winter, its plumage turns to grey-brown upper parts and a grey-white chest and belly, losing its patch. In flight, it shows a pale bar on its pointed wings. Its bill is long, slightly down-curved and black. Dunlins are often seen in very large flocks, both in flight and gathering at feeding grounds.
Length: 17-19cm.

**VOICE** A shrill call and a trilling song.
**HABITAT** Prefers wet grasslands and upland moors for breeding, can also be found on saltmarshes, coastal pools and shallow inland lakes.
**NESTING** Lays 4 olive-buff eggs in a ground nest covered with vegetation.
**RANGE** Breeds in Arctic region, particularly Iceland, northern Scandinavia and the Baltic. Winters in more southerly areas of Europe, including Britain.

# GREEN SANDPIPER (TRINGA OCHROPUS)

**VOICE** Makes a high-pitched 'tweet weet weet' call.

**HABITAT** Prefers woods and forests near to marshland for breeding and feeds in freshwater areas, including sewage works.

**NESTING** Lays 4 greenish eggs with brown spots in a tree nest.

**RANGE** Breeds in northern Europe, particularly Scandinavia and western Russia, migrating west and south. Commonly found in southern Britain.

Smaller and dumpier than its cousin the redshank, the green sandpiper has dark, olive-brown plumage on its upper parts, marked with light spots. Its throat and breast are white with dense dark streaks and its belly and rump are white. It has a dark tail with white bars. Its legs are green and relatively short. When flying, its white, squarish rump contrasts boldly with its dark back and wings. It has a white streak in front of its eye and its bill is straight, long and black. It can be seen constantly bobbing up and down. Length: 23cm.

# (ACTITIS HYPOLEUCOS) SANDPIPER

The sandpiper, often called the common sandpiper, is a small, slim wader with short legs and a short, straight bill. Its head, breast and upper parts are an olive-brown colour, delicately streaked with dark brown. The brown patch on its breast is separated from the wing by a wedge of white plumage which extends up from the white belly. Its relatively long tail is dark and shows white edge feathers when in flight. It flies with stiff, bowed wings which also show a thin white wing bar. Its legs are yellow-green and it can often be seen in a horizontal position, bobbing up and down as it feeds.
Length: 18-20cm.

**VOICE** A high-pitched and shrill call.

**HABITAT** Prefers fast-flowing streams, upland rivers, inland lakes, sewage farms and sheltered estuaries.

**NESTING** Lays 4 creamy eggs with dark spots in a grass-lined scrape near to a river bank.

**RANGE** Found across northern and central Europe, with some wintering in Africa.

# REDSHANK (TRINGA TOTANUS)

**VOICE** Loud, fluting flight call.
**HABITAT** Prefers saltmarshes, coasts and estuaries as well as inland freshwater lakes and reservoirs.
**NESTING** 4 variously coloured eggs are laid in a scrape within vegetation.
**RANGE** Across Iceland and Scandinavia down towards Spain and central Europe. Some birds winter as far south as Africa.

The redshank is a medium-sized wader with distinctive bright red legs. During the breeding season, its upper parts are brownish with dark speckles, becoming a slightly paler brown-grey for the rest of the year. Its underparts are white with dark streaks. In flight, its white rump extends up the back to form a 'v' shape and its wings show broad white edges. Its short tail is white with dark grey bars. The redshank's legs are long, as is its bill, which is red with a black tip. Many seen in Britain are resident but during the summer their numbers swell as migrating birds arrive from Iceland. Length approx: 28cm.

# GREENSHANK (TRINGA NEBULARIA)

A slim, grey wader with long legs and a long, upturned bill, the greenshank is slightly taller than its cousin the redshank. Its upper parts are grey, flecked with black and white. Its breast is pale grey and speckled, as is its head, and it has a white belly. Its wings in flight are dark grey above and it shows a long white 'v' up its back from the rump. Its tail has several dark bars and a dark tip. As its name suggests, its long legs are a bold yellow-green. Juveniles tend to be more brown. Length: 30-31cm.

**Voice** A loud, ringing 'tew tew'.

**Habitat** Boggy moorland, pools and lakes. Often found on reservoirs, gravel pits and sewage farms.

**Nesting** Lays 4 buffy eggs in a hidden ground nest, marked with boulder or branch.

**Range** Breeds across northern Europe, including Scotland and Scandinavia, heads to southern Europe during the winter, many arriving in south-western England, Wales and Ireland.

# TURNSTONE
## (ARENARIA INTERPRES)

As its name suggests, this chunky little wader uses its short upturned bill to turn over stones in order to find food. The turnstone has a large head on a stout body and short orange legs. During the early summer months its head is strongly patterned in black and white, with a mottled black and white crown and a black stripe running through the eye. Its upper parts are a tortoiseshell pattern, with chestnut, black and buff feathers. Its belly and rump are white, separated from the head by a black chest band. In flight it shows a bold white wing bar and a white patch on its back. Its winter plumage is browner and more mottled, and the markings on its head and neck become much less defined.

Length approx: 23cm.

**Voice** A chuckling and twittering.
**Habitat** Usually found on coastlines. Prefers rocky and sandy shores, also found on tidal mud.
**Nesting** Lays 3-4 green, brown-mottled eggs in a shallow ground depression.
**Range** Breeds in far north and Arctic, heads into northern coastal Europe for the winter.

# BLACK-TAILED GODWIT (LIMOSA LIMOSA)

**VOICE** A 'wick-a, wick-a' call.
**HABITAT** Often found on estuaries and coastal lagoons, breeds on wet grassland and marshes.
**NESTING** Lays 4 olive eggs with brown speckles in a grass-lined hollow.
**RANGE** Breeding birds from Iceland and northern Europe head south towards Africa, although many spend the winter in the UK.

A large wader, the black-tailed godwit has particularly long legs and a long straight bill. Its back and upper wings are mottled grey-brown and during the summer the feathers develop black centres. Also at this time, its head, neck and chest are a bright chestnut colour. It has dark stripes on its flanks, and its belly and rump are white. Its plumage fades to grey out of the breeding season. Its long bill is pinkish at the base with a black tip. In flight, its long pointed wings show a broad white wing bar and there is a black bar at the end of the white tail.
Length: 38-41cm.

# (NUMENIUS PHAEOPUS) WHIMBREL

The whimbrel is a large wader with long legs and a long bill that curves downwards at the end. It is very similar to a curlew, although slightly smaller. It has dark brown, speckled plumage on its upper parts, while its underparts are whitish with brown chevron markings on the throat and chest that fade to white on the belly and rump. Its small head bears a pattern of dark stripes; one runs through the eye with a contrasting white brow above. Its bill and legs are both slate grey. When flying, the white rump extends up the back in a 'v' shape between the wings. Length: 38-43cm.

**Voice** A rapidly repeated, whistling note.

**Habitat** Prefers shorelines, estuaries and coastal lagoons and is often seen inland on grassland and fields when breeding.

**Nesting** Lays 4 olive, brown-spotted eggs in a grass-lined hollow.

**Range** Breeds in Iceland, northern Scandinavia and Siberia, visiting central and southern Europe, including Britain, during the winter migration to Africa.

# RUFF (PHILOMACHUS PUGNAX)

**VOICE** Usually silent.
**HABITAT** Prefers water meadows and marshes, muddy edges of lakes and pools.
**NESTING** Lays 4 pale green eggs, blotched with brown, in a grass-lined hollow.
**RANGE** Breeds in northern Europe; most birds migrate to Africa during the winter.

A medium-sized wader, the male ruff is substantially larger than the female and both have a proportionally small head on a long neck. During the winter, the ruff is a nondescript brown-grey, with paler chest and belly. Its bill is relatively short and slightly downcurved, and its legs are either orange or a yellow-green shade. In flight it shows faint wing bars and white patches on the sides of its black tail. During the summer the male grows huge, dramatic feathers around its head and neck. This display plumage is completely black, white or chestnut and its face becomes red-brown. Length: 23-29cm.

# (GALLINAGO GALLINAGO) SNIPE

The snipe is a round and dumpy wader with short legs and a very long bill. Its upper parts are dark brown, marked with striking black and white bars. The head is patterned with bold black and white stripes. Its throat and belly are white, but its breast has delicate brown chevron bars, and its flanks are also marked with bars. When flying, its pointed wings show a white edge and its tail appears short and round. Its back has a double white 'v' marking. Its tail feathers vibrate in flight to produce a drumming sound. Length: 27cm.

**Voice** A rasping call.

**Habitat** Prefers marshes, lagoons, wet pasture and shallow pools, anywhere where it can probe the mud and soft ground with its bill.

**Nesting** Lays 4 olive or brown blotched eggs in a grass-lined hollow, often near water.

**Range** Breeds throughout northern Europe, with many birds from Scandinavia and north-eastern Europe migrating south.

# WOODCOCK (SCOLOPAX RUSTICOLA)

**VOICE** Harsh croaking.
**HABITAT** Prefers deciduous woodland, often marshy with open glades and dense ground cover.
**NESTING** 4 buff eggs, thickly blotched in grey and chestnut, are laid in a hollow lined with dead leaves.
**RANGE** Breeds across northern and central Europe, with some birds migrating south-east towards Asia and China.

The woodcock is a large and dumpy wader with short legs and a very long bill. It has brown, mottled plumage which acts as very effective camouflage. Its upper feathers are a combination of black, brown, chestnut and buff and its underparts are buff with dark barring. It has a black crown crossed with pale brown lines. A ground dweller, its eyes are large and placed high on its head to enable it to spot danger. In flight, its broad wings are rounded and it shows a silvery tip to its tail. It holds its long dark bill pointing downwards. Length approx: 34cm.

# (NUMENIUS ARQUATA) CURLEW

Britain's largest breeding wader, the curlew is common and widespread. It has long grey legs and a very long, downward-curving bill. Its plumage is mainly grey-brown, with darker speckles on its upper parts. Its head and neck are streaked grey. The grey markings on its throat, breast and belly fade to white on its rump. When flying, its long pointed wings are darker at the ends. Its white rump extends up its back to form a deep 'v' and its tail is barred in black and white. The female has a longer bill than the male. Length: 53-58cm.

**Voice** A bubbling and trilling song.
**Habitat** Prefers coastal areas, mudflats, saltmarshes, estuaries and open shores.
**Nesting** Lays 4 green eggs with brown blotches in a ground hollow.
**Range** Breeds across northern and central Europe, winters in southern Europe.

# GREAT SKUA (CATHARACTA SKUA)

**VOICE** Usually silent; loud barking call when disturbed.

**HABITAT** Spends most time out at sea; breeds on rocky islands and coastal moors.

**NESTING** Lays 2 olive-brown eggs on the ground to be incubated by both parents.

**RANGE** Breeds in Iceland, Norway, north Russia, northern Scotland and Northern Isles, migrates towards southern Atlantic coasts.

A very large and aggressive seabird, the great skua is heavy with broad wings, a stout bill and a proportionally short tail. Its plumage is a speckled chocolate brown in colour, with the upper parts often being darker than those below. During the summer its feathers can become paler. In flight, its wings show bright white flashes both above and below. It has a very dark, wedge-shaped tail. It feeds on smaller birds and will also harass gannets, forcing them to regurgitate in order to steal their food. Length: 58-61cm.

# (LARUS CANUS) COMMON GULL

A small and delicate gull, the common gull has a neat round head and a relatively short bill. Its black eye can give the impression of a gentle bird. It has a blue-grey back and in winter its usually white head is streaked with brownish-grey. The narrow grey wings have a black tip, marked with white spots, and its underparts are white. It has yellow-green legs and a yellow bill which becomes dull during the winter; its square tail is white. Although not as common as its name suggests, it can often be seen following ploughs in the countryside.
Length: 40-42cm.

**VOICE** Mewing and chuckling.
**HABITAT** Often found inland; breeds near lakes, bogs and marshes as well as on coastal sites. It can be seen on farmland and playing fields.
**NESTING** Lays 3 pale green, brown-spotted eggs in a grass nest on the ground.
**RANGE** Found across northern Europe from Iceland towards the Bering Sea.

# BLACK-HEADED GULL
## (LARUS RIDIBUNDUS)

The smallest gull in Britain and Ireland, the black-headed gull is also one of the commonest. During the summer it has a chocolate brown hood that does not extend beyond its face. This disappears in winter, to be replaced by a dark spot behind the eye. The rest of its plumage is predominantly white and grey. In flight, its wings are very white along the front edge with dark feathers on the underside at the outer edge. Its bill and legs are bright red during the breeding season, becoming dull grey during the rest of the year. The black-headed gull is often seen inland, and wrongly assumed to be a seagull. Length: 35-38cm.

**VOICE** Harsh nasal call.
**HABITAT** Found on coastal marshes, freshwater lakes and marshes, reservoirs, urban pools, ploughed fields, car parks, playgrounds and rubbish tips.
**NESTING** 2-3 olive-brown eggs with brown and purple blotches are laid in a nest on the marshes or on a lake island.
**RANGE** Found throughout temperate Eurasia. Breeds across northern Europe, from Iceland to the Bering Sea, with many birds wintering on western coasts.

# GREAT BLACK-BACKED GULL (LARUS MARINUS)

**VOICE** Mostly silent.
**HABITAT** Spends much of its time at sea. Breeds on cliffs, marshes, lakes and coastal moors. Also visits habours, fields, sewage works and rubbish tips.
**NESTING** Lays 2-3 olive, brown-spotted eggs in a seaweed nest on the ground or on a rocky stack.
**RANGE** Found around coasts of northern Europe and Scandinavia, Iceland and north-west Russia.

The great black-backed gull is the largest gull in British waters. It has a heavy build, with a large head and bill, a thick neck and a sturdy body. Its back and wings are black and the wings are edged with white. In winter the white head and neck become streaked with grey. Its powerful yellow bill has an orange spot on the underside and it has flesh-coloured legs. During its first year its plumage is rather more speckled and it has a black band on its tail, which becomes white in adulthood. An extremely aggressive predator, feeding on other birds and mammals, the great black-backed gull is also responsible for clearing beaches of dead wildlife. Length: 68-78cm.

# LESSER BLACK-BACKED GULL (LARUS FUSCUS)

A smaller and slimmer bird than the herring gull, the lesser black-backed gull has longer wings. Its back and wings are slate grey to black; the remainder of its plumage is white. During the winter its head and neck become speckled with grey. In flight, its wings tend to show darker plumage at the tips, with white edges. Although its plumage is similar to the great black-backed gull, it has a proportionally smaller yellow bill with an orange spot near the tip and long yellow legs, rather than pink. Length: 55-67cm.

**VOICE** A loud 'kee ow' call.

**HABITAT** Breeds around the coast on sand dunes, shingle and cliff tops and sometimes rooftops. Can be seen on ploughed fields, rubbish tips and large bodies of water.

**NESTING** Lays 3 olive-brown eggs with darker blotches in a ground hollow.

**RANGE** Found around northern European coasts. Some birds migrate south.

# HERRING GULL (LARUS ARGENTATUS)

**VOICE** Wailing and clucking noises.
**HABITAT** Found in most coastal areas, rubbish tips, fields, lakes and reservoirs.
**NESTING** Lays 2-3 pale green, brown-blotched eggs in a scrape among dunes or on rooftops.
**RANGE** Mainly northern Europe, from Iceland across to Scandinavia and Russia.

A large and noisy bird, the herring gull is the most common gull in Britain. It has a light grey back and wings, with black and white spotted wing tips. Its head, neck and underparts are white, with the head developing grey speckles during winter. In flight, its wings are long and broad and its white tail has a square end. Its large bill is yellow with an orange spot near the slightly hooked tip. The legs and feet are flesh pink. It nests in noisy colonies and is a bold scavenger, following boats and approaching people, resulting in its being considered a pest. Length: 56-66cm.

# (RISSA TRIDACTYLA) KITTIWAKE

A neat and graceful medium-sized gull, the kittiwake spends almost all of its time out at sea. Its back and upper wings are a blue-grey; the remainder of its plumage is pure white. In flight, its wings are long and narrow with triangular black wing tips, and its tail is slightly forked. Unlike other gulls, the wings have no white spots. Juvenile birds have a black 'w' mark across their wings and a black stripe across the nape of the neck. Its bill is relatively slender and yellow, and its legs are black with powerful feet and claws for cliff roosting. Length: 38-40cm.

**VOICE** A repeated 'kitti waak' call.

**HABITAT** Breeds on steep cliff walls, some buildings and piers. Otherwise spends most of its time out at sea.

**NESTING** Lays 2 creamy, brown-speckled eggs in a well-constructed nest on a cliff face.

**RANGE** Breeds on coasts of northern Europe, from Iceland across to Scandinavia and Russia. Many winter on waters further south, including the Mediterranean.

# LITTLE GULL (LARUS MINUTUS)

**VOICE** A repeated 'kek kek kek' call.

**HABITAT** Breeds on freshwater marshes. Winters at sea, although can be found on estuaries and lakes inland.

**NESTING** Lays 2-3 olive, brown-spotted eggs in a reed nest in marsh.

**RANGE** Found around Europe's coastline, with breeding populations based in Russia and Baltics.

The smallest gull, the little gull hardly ever breeds in Britain but it can be seen off eastern coasts during the summer and autumn. Its back and upper wings have pale grey plumage. During the summer it has a black head; this moults during the winter to become a sooty back to the head with a dark smudge behind the eye. Its neck, chest and belly are pure white, as is its tail. Its most marked feature is its dark, almost black underwing, with a thin white edge. Juvenile birds have a black band across the end of the tail and a black 'w' stripe across the wingspan. The little gull has a black bill and red legs. Length: 25-27cm.

# (STERNA ALBIFRONS) LITTLE TERN

The smallest tern in Britain, the little tern is a third smaller than the common tern with a proportionally large head and bill. Its back and wings are pale grey and the rest of its body plumage is white. The back of its head and its crown are black; there is a black stripe through its eye but it has a contrasting white forehead at all times. Its long, narrow wings beat very rapidly and it hovers like a kingfisher. Its bill is bright yellow with a black tip, and it has orange legs. Length: 22-24cm.

**Voice** A shrill, repeated call.
**Habitat** Breeds on shingle or sandy coasts in colonies. Can be found along rivers and on lakes.
**Nesting** Lays 2-3 olive eggs, blotched with brown, in a scrape on sand or shingle.
**Range** Found along European coasts, except those in far north. Winters off African coast.

# COMMON TERN (STERNA HIRUNDO)

**VOICE** A loud, harsh 'kee ah' call.
**HABITAT** Breeds on shingle and sandy beaches and most other coastal sites. Can be found inland on reservoirs, often nesting on man-made rafts. During winter is mainly coastal.
**NESTING** 2-3 creamy, heavily brown-spotted eggs laid in a beach scrape.
**RANGE** Breeds in central and eastern Europe and migrates to western Africa during the winter.

As its name suggests, this bird is common and widespread around the coasts of Britain. The common tern is graceful in flight, with long, pointed wings and a deeply forked tail. Its upper parts are silvery grey and the rest of its plumage is grey-white, with a pure white face and neck. It has a black cap and a white forehead, and its bill and legs are orange-red. In flight, its wing tips are a slightly darker grey, and the inner edges appear almost translucent when seen against the light. The juvenile has a browner back and its bill is yellow, getting progressively darker through its first summer.
Length: 31-35cm.

# (STERNA PARADISAEA) ARCTIC TERN

The Arctic tern is very similar in size to the common tern, although slightly smaller and more delicate in appearance. Its distinguishing features are a bright red bill and legs. It has pale grey plumage on both its upper and underparts, which becomes paler on the neck and face. Its rump is white, as is its very long, forked tail. The flight feathers are a slightly darker grey and in flight they can appear translucent against the light. It has a black crown extending down the back of the neck, contrasting with its white cheeks. Length: 33-35cm.

**VOICE** A rasping 'kee kee' call.

**HABITAT** Breeds on sandy or shingle beaches, or on moorlands. Spends the winter at sea.

**NESTING** Lays 2 olive eggs with brown blotches in a bare scrape or hollow.

**RANGE** Breeds in northern Europe, particularly Iceland, Britain and Scandinavia. Migrates long distance to the Antarctic.

# GUILLEMOT (URIA AALGE)

The guillemot is a black and white seabird with a slim head and neck and a long, slender black bill. Its streamlined body is designed for swimming and diving; when resting it tends to stand upright. Its head, back and upper wings are black-brown and its underparts are pure white. Some birds have a white ring around their black eyes. In winter, the front of the neck and the cheeks turn white, with a black streak behind the eye. The guillemot's short, narrow wings have a thin white bar and on the underside are white with black plumage on the edges. Its legs and webbed feet are black. Length: 38-41cm.

**VOICE** Usually silent, growls on the nest.

**HABITAT** Breeds on sheer cliff faces and sloping ledges in colonies. Spends the winter out at sea.

**NESTING** One pear-shaped egg of varying colour is laid on bare rock.

**RANGE** Breeds throughout northern Atlantic and northern seas. Found along northern coastline of Europe with some colonies reaching as far south as the Bay of Biscay.

# (ALCA TORDA) RAZORBILL

A medium-sized seabird, the razorbill is very similar to the guillemot, although slightly smaller, with a short, thick neck and a large head. It has a black head, neck and upper parts and is pure white below. Its black bill is short and thick with a blunt rather than pointed end. It is distinctively marked with a vertical white stripe around the beak and a horizontal white stripe stretching back towards the black eye. Its black upper wings are edged with white and in flight its black tail looks proportionally long, whilst its bill appears blunt. Length: 38-41cm.

**VOICE** Usually silent, whirring and growling on the nest.

**HABITAT** Spends most of its time out at sea. During breeding, prefers rocky coasts and cliffs.

**NESTING** A single pale, oval egg with dark blotches is laid on bare ground on a cliff ledge.

**RANGE** In Europe, breeds on northern coasts, particularly Iceland, Scandinavia and western Britain. Winters in the northern Atlantic.

# PUFFIN
## (FRATERCULA ARCTICA)

A small and chunky auk, the puffin is well known for its black and white plumage and its large colourful bill. Its upper parts are black, as is its neck and crown, and its chest and belly are white. The large face is dusky white and its dark eye is rimmed with red. Its bill is deep and flattened, giving it a triangular appearance, and it is brightly coloured from the tip to the base with red, orange and blue stripes. During the winter, layers are shed from the bill and it becomes slightly smaller and duller. The puffin is usually seen standing upright on its bright orange legs and webbed feet. In flight, its underwing is grey and its black tail has a square end.
Length: 26-29cm.

**VOICE** Growling at breeding site.
**HABITAT** During breeding, it lives on offshore islands and sea cliffs, usually in large colonies. Otherwise, out at sea.
**NESTING** Lays a single white egg in a self-dug burrow or uses an old rabbit hole.
**RANGE** Breeds in north-western Europe, particularly Scandinavia, Britain, north-west France and Iceland. Some migrate towards Mediterranean.

# COLLARED DOVE (STREPTOPELIA DECAOCTO)

**VOICE** An often-heard 'coo coo coo' call.

**HABITAT** Frequently found in urban areas, it prefers farms, gardens and parks, and tends to avoid busier city centres.

**NESTING** Builds a simple nest in a tree or on a building ledge which holds 2 white eggs.

**RANGE** Originally found in the Balkans, the collared dove has successfully spread across central and eastern Europe, from as far south as Greece towards Scandinavia.

A medium-sized dove, the collared dove has a small head and a relatively long, elegant tail. Its back and upper wings are a pale brown-grey colour, its head and underparts are pale pinkish-grey. It has a distinctive black half-collar on the back of its neck. In flight, its wings show blue-grey flight feathers and the tail has a clear white band at the end, which is fanned out during courtship displays. Its bill is black and its legs and feet are a pinkish red. Length: 31-33cm.

# (COLUMBA LIVIA) ROCK DOVE

The ancestor of the feral pigeon, so familiar in towns and cities, the rock dove's plumage can vary. In general, it is a pale blue-grey colour, with a slightly darker head, neck and breast. It has a darker grey tail and flight feathers. Its rump is white and, in flight, its underwings are pale grey. It has two darker grey broad bands across its inner wings, which are apparent when the bird is at rest. The sides of its neck are often an iridescent green and purple. Its bill is small and dark, with a white stripe across the top.
Length: 31-34cm.

**Voice** A gentle cooing.
**Habitat** The true rock dove prefers sea cliffs and rock faces. The feral variety will live around buildings.
**Nesting** Lays 2 white eggs in a nest, either on a cliff or a building ledge.
**Range** Found in central and western Europe. The feral variety is found throughout the world.

# STOCK DOVE (COLUMBA OENAS)

**VOICE** A deep 'oo woo oo woo' call.
**HABITAT** Prefers woodland areas such as parks and wooded farmland. Can also be found on cliffs and old buildings.
**NESTING** Lays 2 white eggs in a nest placed in a tree hole or in a niche of a building or a cliff face.
**RANGE** Found across western Europe, with many birds moving westwards during winter. Half of the European population can be found in the UK.

The stock dove is a compact pigeon similar in size and shape to the rock dove, although slightly slimmer. It has blue-grey plumage, with an iridescent green and purple patch on its neck and a pink blush to its breast. Its plain grey wings have dark edges, most clearly seen when the bird is in flight. Its rump is grey, rather than white like the rock dove's, and its tail has a dark bar at the end. It does have dark wing bars, but unlike those of the rock dove, they are very short and close to the back. Its bill is a dull orange and its legs are flesh pink.
Length: 34cm.

# (COLUMBA PALUMBUS) WOODPIGEON

Britain's largest pigeon, with broad wings, a stocky chest and a long tail. The woodpigeon's plumage is mainly blue-grey with an iridescent green and purple patch on its neck and a pink blush to its breast. It has a white patch on its neck and a white slash on the 'elbow' or bend of its wing. When flying, its darker flight feathers and dark grey tail band can be clearly seen, as can the white patches on its upper wing, which become a crescent-shaped line. The bill is a pinkish orange and it has flesh-coloured legs and feet. Length: 40-42cm.

**VOICE** A loud cooing call.
**HABITAT** Prefers farmland with hedges and trees although can now be found in urban parks and gardens.
**NESTING** Lays 2 white eggs in a thin nest built on tree branches or buildings.
**RANGE** Found across Europe, with eastern populations heading west during winter. British birds tend not to migrate.

# CUCKOO
## (CUCULUS CANORUS)

The cuckoo is a slender, dove-sized bird with a long tail, pointed wings and a small head. Its head, breast and upper parts are blue-grey while its lower breast and belly are white with fine black bars. In flight, its narrow, pointed wings and long tail can make it look like a kestrel. The tail has a slightly rounded end and is tipped with a fine white bar. Females can be slightly browner than the males. Juvenile birds have brown, speckled plumage and white feathers on the back of the head. Length: 32-34cm.

**VOICE** A loud 'cuck-oo' call.

**HABITAT** A variety of habitats. Cuckoos inhabit areas where suitable breeding hosts can be found, from moorland and farmland to wetlands and sand dunes.

**NESTING** Infamous for laying their eggs in the nests of other birds, they quickly leave a single egg in place of one belonging to the host, who then incubates and feeds the fledgling cuckoo.

**RANGE** Breeds throughout Europe. Migrates to central and southern Africa.

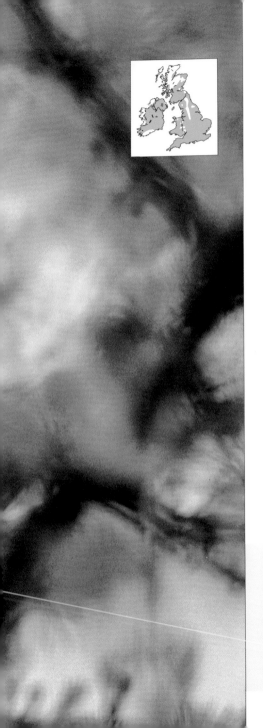

# BARN OWL
## (TYTO ALBA)

The barn owl is a medium-sized owl, with a large head, heart-shaped face, long, slim wings and long legs. The British barn owl has very pale, soft plumage. Its upper parts are a honey brown with delicate grey and white spots. Its underparts can be either pure white or a buff-brown with darker spots. The female tends to have more streaks on her back and some spotting on her breast. The barn owl's face and the underside of its wings are pure white and in flight its wings are rounded. Its large face lacks ear tufts and can change shape. This enables it to spot the slightest movement from possible prey. Its toes and claws are very strong, with a reversible outer toe to aid perching and hunting. A nocturnal hunter, the barn owl is often seen illuminated in the glare of car headlights.
Length: 33-35cm.

**VOICE** Shrieking and screeching calls.
**HABITAT** Prefers open countryside for hunting; nests in barns, deserted buildings and large trees.
**NESTING** Lays 4-7 white eggs in a tree hole, barn or other suitable building.
**RANGE** Found across Europe except Scandinavia.

# LITTLE OWL
(ATHENE NOCTUA)

The smallest owl in the UK, commonly seen in daylight. The little owl has a plump and squat shape, with a flat head and short tail. Its upper parts are grey-brown with large white spots and streaks on the head and neck. Its underparts are much lighter, almost grey, with darker streaks on the breast and belly. Its underwing is pale and barred, and its rounded wings beat quickly in flight. Its face is pale grey and it has large yellow eyes under white 'eyebrows', giving it a fierce expression. Length: 21-23cm.

**VOICE** A high-pitched 'kew kew' call.
**HABITAT** Prefers open countryside for hunting, but close to trees and hedges for nesting.
**NESTING** Lays 3-5 white eggs in a tree hole or building crevice.
**RANGE** Found across Europe throughout the year, except in Scandinavia and Russia.

# LONG-EARED OWL (ASIO OTUS)

**VOICE** A low 'oo oo oo' call.

**HABITAT** Prefers dense conifer woodland close to open countryside. During winter can be found near to the coast.

**NESTING** Lays 4-5 white eggs in an abandoned nest, usually in a tree.

**RANGE** Found across Europe throughout the year, visiting Scandinavia and Russia during the summer.

The long-eared owl is a medium-sized owl, with a relatively slim body and long wings. Its most distinguishing features are its long ear tufts, which it raises when alarmed, and its large orange eyes. Its plumage is mainly buff-brown with streaks; the upper parts are darker with heavy bars and spots in a variety of shades. The underparts, including the wings, are lighter buff with fine bars. Its face is oval and a warm buff colour, and the ear tufts are streaked with dark brown. Slim and long when upright and alarmed, at rest the long-eared owl fluffs up its feathers and flattens its ears. It also keeps its ears flat in flight. A strictly nocturnal bird, it is rarely seen. Length: 35-37cm.

# (ASIO FLAMMEUS) SHORT-EARED OWL

A medium-sized brown owl, with a large round head and short ear tufts. The short-eared owl's plumage is heavily streaked brown, with darker spots and streaks on a chestnut and buff base. Its underparts are slightly paler, but just as heavily barred. In flight, it shows long, narrow and round-ended wings with dark patches on the 'elbow' or bend. Its face is a pale buff colour and it has large, prominent, yellow eyes. It hunts during daylight and glides low over the ground like a harrier. Length: 35-38cm.

**VOICE** Usually silent, occasional deep hooting.

**HABITAT** Prefers open country such as moorland, heaths and sand dunes.

**NESTING** Lays 4-8 white eggs in an unlined ground hollow covered with vegetation.

**RANGE** Found across Eurasia, including Iceland and Scandinavia; birds from northern Europe and Russia migrate towards south-western Europe, including Britain.

# TAWNY OWL
## (STRIX ALUCO)

A plump owl, with a large, flat, round head and a compact body. The tawny owl's plumage can vary, but is usually a rich brown above with dark streaks and bars, and paler feathers on its underparts with dark streaking. Its face is usually brown with a ring of darker feathers framing it. Its eyes are large and dark. In flight, the tawny owl has long, broad, rounded wings and it flies quickly and quietly. Its short neck and flat face are distinctive features when seen from below. Length: 37-39cm.

**VOICE** A distinctive hooting call.
**HABITAT** Prefers woodland for breeding, but can be found on farmland and in gardens.
**NESTING** Lays 2-4 white eggs in a natural or man-made hole.
**RANGE** Found throughout Europe, except Iceland and Scandinavia.

# NIGHTJAR (CAPRIMULGUS EUROPAEUS)

**VOICE** A purring call made in flight.
**HABITAT** Prefers heathland, moors and other areas of bare ground for nesting.
**NESTING** 2 white eggs with brown spots are laid amongst leaves on the ground to be incubated by both parents.
**RANGE** Widespread across Europe during the summer; winters in Africa.

The nightjar is a small bird, with a large head, pointed wings, long tail and small bill and feet. Its plumage is mainly grey-brown, mottled and streaked in order to provide camouflage. It also has white markings on the edges of its long, barred tail. In flight, its wings show white edging on the outer feathers and a small white patch on the tips. Although its bill is very small, its mouth, when open, is relatively huge and edged with bristles. It flies silently with its mouth gaping in order to catch insects. A nocturnal bird, the nightjar is rarely seen.
Length: 26-28cm.

# (APUS APUS) SWIFT

A small aerial bird with a relatively short body and long, pointed, sickle-shaped wings. The swift's body, wings and tail are a dark brown, almost black, without any markings. It has a white chin and a small black bill, which opens to reveal a large mouth designed to catch insects in flight. Its tail is short and pointed and its short, weak legs and feet are adapted for clinging onto buildings and vertical surfaces. It never perches, and grounded swifts struggle to regain the air. A fast and erratic flyer, the swift spends most of its life in flight. Length: 16-17cm.

**Voice** Shrieking and screaming in flight.

**Habitat** Aerial, over a variety of habitats. In Britain, tends to breed only in buildings.

**Nesting** Builds a shallow nest of straw and saliva under the eaves of a building or in a crevice.

**Range** Visits Europe, including British Isles, during the summer; migrates to tropical Africa.

# KINGFISHER
(ALCEDO ATTHIS)

A small bird with short wings and tail, large head and a long, pointed bill. The kingfisher has distinctively colourful plumage which can appear muted when seen in shade. Its back is a bright turquoise, with blue wings and a blue speckled crown. Its cheeks are a chestnut red, as is its chest, belly and rump. It has a white patch on its throat and a white stripe on its neck below the cheek. The male's bill is black; the female's has a red patch on the lower part. It often hovers above water before diving to catch fish.
Length: 15-17cm.

**Voice** A repeated, chattering 'cheek' sound.
**Habitat** Freshwater rivers, canals and lakes are preferred for breeding. Can often be found at coastal sites in winter.
**Nesting** Lays 4-8 white eggs in a nest burrowed into the ground on a river bank.
**Range** Found across western and central Europe, including England, Wales and Ireland.

# GREAT SPOTTED WOODPECKER
## (DENDROCOPOS MAJOR)

**VOICE** A loud 'kik kik' call. Also drums on tree branch with its bill.
**HABITAT** Prefers large trees, in either woodland or cultivated areas.
**NESTING** Lays 3-8 white eggs in an unlined tree hole which it excavates.
**RANGE** Found across Europe throughout the year, although absent from Ireland, northern Scotland and northern Scandinavia.

A medium-sized woodpecker, about the size of a blackbird, with a strong bill, short, pointed tail and broad, rounded wings. The great spotted has black upper parts marked with white spots on the wings and large white patches on the 'shoulders'. Its crown is black, extending down the nape of the neck, but its face is white, marked with a black moustache running across the cheeks. The male has a red patch on the nape of the neck which the female lacks. Both sexes have a red patch under the tail. Its underparts are a creamy white.
Length: 22-23cm.

# LESSER SPOTTED WOODPECKER
(DENDROCOPOS MINOR)

The lesser spotted woodpecker is the smallest and least common woodpecker in Britain. Its upper parts are black with white bars and it lacks the large white shoulder patch seen on the great spotted woodpecker. The male has a red crown and black neck, with its white face marked with a black stripe. The female has similar black and white markings but a creamy crown, instead of red. Both sexes have white underparts with black streaks. It has no red feathers under its tail, unlike the great spotted woodpecker. Length: 13-15cm.

**Voice** A shrill 'pee pee' call. Knocks gently on tree branches with its bill.

**Habitat** Breeds in wooded areas and can be found in hedgerows and gardens.

**Nesting** Excavates nest holes in trees; lays 3-8 white eggs in the unlined cavity.

**Range** Found across central Europe throughout the year. In Britain found only in England and Wales.

# GREEN WOODPECKER
## (PICUS VIRIDIS)

The green woodpecker is the largest woodpecker found in the UK, with a stocky body, long bill and relatively short tail. Its upper parts are grey-green and its underparts are a pale, buffy green. Its green flight feathers are spotted with white and it has a yellow rump. The most striking feature is its crimson crown. It has a black patch around its eye that extends to its bill and a red streak bordered by black beneath the eye. Often seen feeding on the ground, it uses its bill to pierce the earth and then extends its sticky tongue to extract insects. Length: 28-33cm.

**VOICE** A ringing laughing call. Rarely drums.
**HABITAT** Prefers deciduous woodland for nesting, although can be seen in open farmland and parks.
**NESTING** Lays 4-9 white eggs in a tree hole excavated by both birds.
**RANGE** Found across Europe throughout the year, although not seen in Ireland or north-western Scotland.

# WOODLARK (LULLULA ARBOREA)

**VOICE** A musical, fluty song.

**HABITAT** Prefers open grassland and open woodland for breeding. Can often be found with skylarks on fields.

**NESTING** Lays 3-5 grey-white eggs with brown spots in a covered ground nest.

**RANGE** Found across Europe during the summer, with eastern birds moving into western Europe. In Britain is restricted to southern England.

The woodlark is a small lark, smaller than the skylark, with a short tail and a delicate bill. Its plumage is brown and streaked on the upper parts; the underparts are white with brown streaks on the breast. Its crown is streaked and it has a white eye stripe that extends across the head and meets at the nape of the neck. Its cheeks are buff and it has a small crest which is occasionally raised. In flight it has broad, rounded wings, with a black and white mark near the 'elbow'. Its short, square tail is finely edged with white. Length approx: 15cm.

# (ALAUDA ARVENSIS) SKYLARK

Often heard before it is seen, the skylark's extravagant song is not matched by its appearance. Brown upper parts are streaked with black and it has a paler underside and a boldly streaked breast. Its chestnut crown is topped with a small crest. In flight the wings are edged with white feathers, a feature that sets skylarks apart from most other larks, as do the longer tail feathers touched with white. Rarely seen near trees, they rise from their ground nests emitting a high-pitched, musical song which continues as they hover and then plummet down with folded wings. The rapid decline in their numbers over recent decades has stimulated much research into the effect of modern intensive farming on birds. Length: 18-19cm.

**VOICE** Call is a metallic 'chree' or 'chreeoo' with an almost constant melody of trills and whistles.

**HABITAT** Most open areas including grasslands, cereal fields, moorland, dunes and saltmarshes.

**NESTING** A small, shallow, grass nest, placed in a hollow among vegetation, holding up to 5 greenish-white eggs.

**RANGE** Britain and Ireland as well as most of Eurasia, with wintering populations in western Europe, the Middle East and China.

# SWALLOW (HIRUNDO RUSTICA)

**Voice** A high, twittering call.

**Habitat** Found in any area where there are plenty of insects: near to cattle in open countryside. Can also be found nesting in buildings, although usually rural.

**Nesting** 3-6 white eggs with brown and grey spots are laid in a mud cup off the ground, often in a building or a bridge.

**Range** A summer visitor across Europe. Most birds migrate south; British swallows have been found in South Africa.

Smaller than the similar swift, the swallow is slim with a very long, forked tail, long, pointed wings and a tiny bill. Its upper parts are a dark, iridescent blue and its chest and belly are creamy white. It has a dark blue chest band and its forehead and throat are brick red. When flying it shows white patches on the underside of its tail and its underwings are pale at the base with darker flight feathers. An expert flyer, it spends most of its time in the air, feeding on insects in flight. Length: 17-19cm.

# (RIPARIA RIPARIA) SAND MARTIN

The smallest member of the swallow and martin family, the sand martin has a slender body and long, pointed wings. Its tail is only slightly forked. Its upper parts are plain brown and it is pure white below, with a brown breast band separating its white face and chest. In flight, its wings are relatively narrow and it flies with speed and agility. Unlike other swallows and martins, it tends to avoid urban areas and nests in large colonies. Length: 11-12cm.

**VOICE** A nasal twittering.
**HABITAT** Breeds in sandy banks and quarries. Often seen flying over water.
**NESTING** Lays 3-7 white eggs in a straw nest at the end of a nest chamber which it has excavated.
**RANGE** Found across Europe during the summer; migrates to Saharan Africa.

# HOUSE MARTIN
## (DELICHON URBICA)

Smaller than its relative the swallow, the house martin is plump with short, pointed wings and a shorter forked tail. Its upper parts are a glossy blue-black, with pure white underparts. Its rump is a conspicuous white, and it has white feathers on its legs and feet. Its crown and face above the dark eye are also blue-black, and its throat and cheeks white. A fluttering flyer, it spends most of its time in the air, feeding on insects.
Length: 12-13cm.

**VOICE** A soft, twittering song.
**HABITAT** Common in urban areas, found nesting on buildings. Some still nest on cliffs.
**NESTING** Lays 2-6 white eggs in a nest cup made of mud attached to a vertical surface.
**RANGE** Found across Europe in the summer, migrates to central and southern Africa.

# MEADOW PIPIT (ANTHUS PRATENSIS)

**Voice** A high, squeaking song which ends with a trill.

**Habitat** Prefers open countryside such as grassland, meadows, pastures and moorland. Can often be seen in grassy urban areas.

**Nesting** Lays 3-6 brownish, spotted eggs in a ground nest lined with grass.

**Range** Found across central and eastern Europe, with eastern birds moving south for the winter. The UK population moves from the north to the south of the country during winter.

The meadow pipit is a small, slender songbird with a delicate bill. Its upper parts are buff, streaked with brown, and its underparts are creamy, also streaked with brown on its chest and flanks, with a white belly. Its brown-streaked, longish tail is edged with white and bobs constantly. Its face is a plain brown, with a white streak above the eye. Its legs and feet are dark pink, with lighter pink legs on juvenile birds. Its flight can be quite jerky and it often drifts towards the ground with its wings half open. Length: 14-15cm.

# (ANTHUS SPINOLETTA) ROCK PIPIT

The rock pipit is larger than the meadow pipit, with a stocky body and sturdier bill. Its plumage is greyer than that of its relative and its upper parts are heavily streaked greybrown. Birds that are resident in the UK have white underparts; those that visit from Scandinavia during the winter have grey plumage below. Both have dark streaks on the chest and flanks, although these are more mottled than those of the meadow pipit. Its outer tail feathers are grey rather than white and its legs are dark. It is often seen running over coastal rocks looking for food. Length: 16-17cm.

**VOICE** A single note, 'peep'.
**HABITAT** Found near the coast on cliffs, rocky beaches and saltmarshes.
**NESTING** Lays 4-6 grey-spotted eggs in a grass-lined nest built in a cliff hole or on the ground.
**RANGE** Found along coast of north-western Europe, including British Isles and Scandinavia.

# TREE PIPIT (ANTHUS TRIVIALIS)

**Voice** A series of trills and repeated notes. Harsher than that of the meadow pipit.

**Habitat** Prefers open woodland, such as parkland, heath and young conifer plantations.

**Nesting** Lays 3-6 speckled eggs in a grass-lined ground nest.

**Range** During the summer is found across Europe with the exception of southern Spain and the Mediterranean. Migrates to Africa for the winter.

The tree pipit is slightly larger than the meadow pipit, with a heavier bill. Like its relative, its upper parts are a heavily streaked brown, and it has a prominent white stripe above the eye. Its underparts are creamy white, with heavy brown streaks on the chest and much finer streaks on the flanks. It is distinguished from its cousin by these markings and by its different voice. It has white edges to its tail feathers and its legs are pink. Length: 15cm.

# (MOTACILLA FLAVA) YELLOW WAGTAIL

A small and slender bird with a medium length tail that it occasionally wags. The male yellow wagtail's plumage can vary slightly according to subspecies, but in general it has yellowy-green plumage on its upper parts and yellow below. Its crown can vary from green to black and it can often show a cheek patch or yellow eyebrow. Its wings have dark flight feathers edged with white and its dark tail is also bordered in white. Its legs, bill and eyes are black. Females have duller plumage than males. Length: 16-17cm.

**VOICE** A ringing, 'tsweep' call.

**HABITAT** During the summer it prefers water meadows, marshes, riversides and pastures.

**NESTING** Lays 4-6 creamy eggs, speckled with brown, in a ground nest covered with vegetation.

**RANGE** Found across Europe during the summer, it migrates to Africa for the winter.

# GREY WAGTAIL
## (MOTACILLA CINEREA)

A slender and graceful wagtail, the grey wagtail has a longer tail than its relatives. Its upper parts are blue-grey, with a white stripe above the eye. Its flight feathers and tail are dark grey, edged with white. The male has a black throat and a white moustache-like streak. Its belly is creamy white and its chest and undertail are lemon yellow, which is brighter in the male than in the female. It has a dark bill and legs. The grey wagtail is often seen running near water in search of food, bobbing its long tail.
Length: 18-19cm.

**VOICE** A melodious, trilling song.
**HABITAT** When breeding, prefers fast-flowing water and can be found in woodland near rivers. Out of season can also be found near lowland rivers, streams, canals and lakes.
**NESTING** 4-6 buff, grey-mottled eggs are laid in a ground nest near to fast-flowing water.
**RANGE** Found across central and western Europe throughout the year.

# PIED WAGTAIL (MOTACILLA ALBA YARRELLII)

**Voice** A sharp single note and the occasional twittering.

**Habitat** When breeding it prefers to be near water such as rivers, lakes and estuaries. Can also be found near coasts, on sewage works and farmland.

**Nesting** Lays 4-7 blue-grey eggs in a nest inside a rock crevice, building or tree hole.

**Range** Found in Britain, southern and western Europe all year round. A summer visitor in eastern Europe and across into Russia; eastern birds migrate southwards.

Similar in size to the grey wagtail, the pied wagtail has a relatively shorter tail. Its back, crown, chest and throat are black. It has a white face and white chest and belly which contrast strongly with its upper parts. Its wings are black and white above with a whitish underside. Its tail is black, edged with white, and is constantly bobbed up and down. The female's plumage is less distinct, and her upper parts are more grey than black. Both have a black bill and dark legs. Length: 18cm.

# (BOMBYCILLA GARRULUS) WAXWING

The waxwing is a small, stocky bird with a plump body, short tail and bill, and short legs. Its plumage is a pinkish brown, slightly darker on its head and back. Its lower back and rump is blue-grey, as is its tail which has a bright yellow tip. Its undertail plumage is chestnut red. Its dark wings are edged with yellow and white markings and it has spiky, waxy, red tips on its flight feathers. Its other distinguishing feature is its generous crest, which is reddish brown. It has a black throat patch or bib, and a black eye 'mask'. In flight, its wing shape resembles that of a starling, broad based and pointed. Length: 18cm.

**Voice** A high-pitched trilling.

**Habitat** Prefers dense pine forests for breeding but can usually be found anywhere where trees and bushes bear berries, including parks and gardens.

**Nesting** Lays 4-6 pale blue-grey eggs in a nest on conifer branches.

**Range** Breeds in northern Scandinavia and Russia, winters in eastern Europe. British visitors are found along eastern coasts and southern Scotland.

# DIPPER
(CINCLUS CINCLUS)

The dipper is a small and dumpy bird with a short tail, short wings and relatively long legs. Its upper parts are a dark brown, almost black, as are its belly and undertail. Its head is a slightly lighter shade of brown. Its throat and breast are white and at close range it shows a reddish band across its upper belly. Its bill is sharp and dark and white eyelids can be seen when it blinks. In flight it has short, rounded wings and when standing it is in constant bobbing motion, often with its tail cocked. Length: 18cm.

**VOICE** A sharp 'zit zit' flight call; song is warbling.

**HABITAT** An aquatic bird, it prefers fast-flowing streams and rivers, where it can be found on exposed rocks and boulders before diving for prey on the river bed.

**NESTING** Lays 3-6 white eggs in large nest built into crevice or on rock face or river bank, often under bridges.

**RANGE** Found across Europe, including Scandinavia, Britain, Spain and southern central Europe. Mostly found in the north and west of the UK.

# WREN
## (TROGLODYTES TROGLODYTES)

**VOICE** A loud warbling song, with a trill.

**HABITAT** Prefers dense woodland with thick undergrowth in which to nest and find food, but can be found in parks and gardens, on moorland and in hedgerows.

**NESTING** Lays 5-6 white eggs with brown spots in a domed nest built into a tree hole or in a rock crevice, bank or even a building.

**RANGE** A widespread resident across Europe; found throughout Britain.

The wren is a very small bird, with a plump body, short wings, neck and tail. Its plumage is mainly brown. The darker chestnut upper parts are barred black and its paler, buff underparts have delicate brown bars, mainly on the flanks. It has a long pale stripe above its black eye. Its narrow tail is frequently cocked and it bobs and moves constantly. The bill is slender and it has relatively long legs. It flies on broad, rounded wings, usually close to the ground.
Length: 9-10cm.

# HEDGE SPARROW/DUNNOCK
## (PRUNELLA MODULARIS)

The hedge sparrow or dunnock is a small grey and brown bird with a needle-sharp bill. Its back and upper wings are reddish brown, streaked with black. Its crown is brown with black streaks and it has a brown-streaked cheek patch. The rest of its plumage is blue-grey, with streaked flanks and a paler belly. In flight, its short wings show a buff wing bar. It has relatively long pink legs and a long brown tail. A ground feeder, it can often be seen shuffling and hopping, searching for food in the undergrowth. Length: 14-15cm.

**VOICE** A high-pitched warbling.
**HABITAT** Prefers thick vegetation and ground cover, such as hedges, thickets and woodland. Can be found in parks and gardens.
**NESTING** Lays 3-6 light blue eggs in a nest built into bush or small tree.
**RANGE** Found across western and central Europe; resident in Britain throughout the year.

# ROBIN
(ERITHACUS RU[

Perhaps Britain's most familiar and popular bird, the robin is small with a variable body shape; it can be round and plump or rather more slender. Its upper parts are a khaki brown and a grey line provides a border around the bright red breast and face plumage. Its underparts are buff coloured, with white feathers extending from the belly to the undertail. It has a relatively long, square-ended tail and long black legs. Its bill is short, sharp and dark and it has large dark eyes. Younger birds lack the distinctive red breast and face, and are more mottled and streaked than the adults. Although associated with Christmas, the robin is widespread all year round and can often be seen and heard in town gardens. Length: 14cm.

**Voice** A high, warbling song, with trembling notes and trills.
**Habitat** Prefers ground with undergrowth; can be found in woodland, hedgerows, parks and gardens.
**Nesting** Lays 5-6 white eggs with brown speckles in a nest hidden in bushes or a nest box.
**Range** Found across western Europe throughout the year; is a summer visitor to eastern and northern Europe.

# NIGHTINGALE (LUSCINIA MEGARHYNCHOS)

**VOICE** A loud and melodious song, with warbling notes finishing in a crescendo.

**HABITAT** It prefers thick foliage and dense undergrowth, so is usually found near bushes, hedges, overgrown ditches and thickets.

**NESTING** 4-5 grey-blue eggs with brown markings are laid in a cup nest among ground vegetation.

**RANGE** Visits western Europe, including the south and east of Britain, during the summer months. Winters in Saharan Africa.

More easily recognized by its song than its appearance, the nightingale is a medium-to-small bird with a thick, pale bill, long, pale legs, pointed wings and a longish tail. Its upper parts are a plain warm brown and its underparts are a paler grey-brown colour. It has a white throat and a white rump. Its rounded tail is a chestnut red and can often be seen cocked. Its dark eye is surrounded by a pale eye ring. A shy bird, its colour provides ample camouflage as it hops through the undergrowth. Length: 16-17cm.

# (PHOENICURUS PHOENICURUS) REDSTART

The redstart is a slim bird with a long tail and relatively long wings. The male has blue-grey upper parts with a pale grey crown and a white forehead which extends above the eye. Its underparts are pale orange and it has a black face and throat. Its tail and rump are bright orange. The female has grey-brown upper parts and buff-coloured underparts with a reddish tail. On both sexes, the tail is seen constantly quivering. The redstart has dark legs, a dark bill and dark eyes. It spends most of its time in the lower branches of trees, fluttering and jumping from branch to branch, and occasionally to the ground, in search of food. Length: 14cm.

**Voice** A loud, metallic, warbling call.

**Habitat** A woodland bird, it prefers mature forests and woods, hedges, scrubland and parks.

**Nesting** Lays 6-7 pale blue eggs in a cup nest in a tree hole or bank.

**Range** A summer visitor to western and central Europe, it winters in central Africa.

# STONECHAT (SAXICOLA TORQUATA)

**VOICE** Its call is a metallic 'whit sac sac'
which sounds like stones being
smacked together.
**HABITAT** Found in low vegetation such
as bushes, gorse, hedges and
thickets.
**NESTING** Lays 5-6 blue eggs speckled
with brown in a cup nest on the
ground.
**RANGE** Found across western Europe,
although in eastern Europe is only a
summer visitor.

Slightly smaller than a robin, the stonechat is
a small, plump bird with a round head, short
neck and short, pointed wings. The male has
dark brown upper parts which can be
slightly mottled. Its head is black with a
contrasting white patch on the neck. Its
underparts are orange fading to white on the
belly. The female has similar markings but is
less distinct and browner above, without the
black head. In flight, its broad, short,
rounded wings show a white bar and it also
has a white rump. It has dark eyes, a sharp,
dark bill and slender dark legs. Its tail is
square at the end and edged with black.
Length: 12-13cm.

# (SAXICOLA RUBETRA) WHINCHAT

Smaller in size than a robin and slimmer than the stonechat, the whinchat has long wings, a thicker bill and a flat head. The male has darker plumage than the female in summer, with brown, streaky upper parts and a dark face. Both have a white stripe extending from the bill over and above the eye and the male has a white moustache-like streak. Its underparts are a warm buff colour and the male has a slightly chestnut-coloured breast and throat. Its square-ended tail is dark with white patches on the sides. In flight, its wings show a white 'shoulder' patch. Length: 12-13cm.

**VOICE** A sharp 'tic tic' call and a warbling song.
**HABITAT** Prefers open ground such as moorland, grassland, heaths and mountain plains. It does need obvious perches from which to hunt.
**NESTING** Lays 5-7 blue eggs with brown speckles in a ground nest.
**RANGE** A summer visitor to most of western and northern Europe; migrates to central Africa.

# WHEATEAR (OENANTHE OENANTHE)

**VOICE** A harsh 'cak cak' call and a warbling song.
**HABITAT** Prefers open country such as moorland and upland pastures. It requires rocky ground for breeding and so can often be found in coastal areas.
**NESTING** Lays 5-6 pale blue eggs in a ground hole amongst stones or rocks.
**RANGE** Found across Europe during the breeding season; all birds migrate to east Africa.

Larger than a robin, the wheatear is a sturdy, upright bird. Its crown and back are blue-grey and its wings are black. It has a black eye mask and a white eyebrow stripe. Its throat and breast are buffy orange fading to white on the belly. In flight it shows a white rump and its square-ended tail is edged with black, with a black stripe running up the centre. The female has mainly pale brown, mottled plumage, with less distinctive face markings. Her tail has a pattern similar to the male's. Both have black bill, eyes and legs. Length: 14-15cm.

# (TURDUS PILARIS) FIELDFARE

A large thrush, although smaller than the mistle thrush. The fieldfare is a plump and stocky upright bird, with a long tail and broad, rounded wings. Its head, nape and rump are pale grey, while its back and wings are chestnut brown. Its tail is black. Its underparts are buff coloured, with dark speckles and chevrons, fading to white on its belly. Although its face is grey, it has a dark smudge around the eye and a white eyebrow streak. Its dark eye is surrounded by a yellow ring and it has a yellow bill with a black tip. Length: 25-26cm.

**VOICE** A harsh 'chack chack' call and a warbling song with chuckles.

**HABITAT** Prefers open countryside and, as its name suggests, can often be seen over fields and moorland. Breeds in woodland and so needs to be near trees. Common in parks and gardens.

**NESTING** Lays 5-6 pale blue eggs with brown spots in a tree nest.

**RANGE** Breeds in central and eastern Europe and winters in warmer western and southern Europe, including Britain.

# BLACKBIRD
## (TURDUS MERULA)

A familiar garden bird, found across Britain, the blackbird is a relatively large songbird, with a sturdy body, round head and medium-length tail. As its name suggests, its plumage is completely black, but only in the adult male. It has a distinctive yellow bill and a yellow ring around its eye. The female is dark brown above with paler brown underparts that are mottled and vaguely speckled. She lacks the yellow bill of the male. Juvenile blackbirds are brown-black above and mottled brown below, with a darker bill which gradually fades. In flight, its broad, rounded wings droop slightly, especially before landing. It can often be seen sunbathing with its wings spread and its feathers ruffled, or searching for earthworms, creating as much mess as possible. Length: 24-25cm.

**VOICE** A loud alarm rattle and a fluting, melodious song.
**HABITAT** Originally woodland and heathland, can now be found on farmland, golf courses and in gardens. Prefers short grassy areas for feeding, with bushes and trees for roosting and cover.
**NESTING** Lays 4-5 pale blue eggs in a grass and mud nest built in a tree.
**RANGE** Abundant across Europe throughout the year, with Scandinavian and Russian birds migrating towards Africa.

# SONG THRUSH
## (TURDUS PHILOMELOS)

The song thrush is a small songbird, commonly seen and heard in urban gardens; it is smaller than a blackbird, with a shorter tail and bill and a more slender body. Its upper parts are warm brown. Its chest and flanks are a sandy buff and the underparts are white with small black spots extending from the throat to the belly. In flight it shows a faint buff wing bar and its underwing is a buff colour. It has small, dark eyes, a grey bill and pale legs. Song thrushes are unique in using stones as 'anvils' to smash open snail shells. Length: 23cm.

**VOICE** A fluting, repeated whistle song.
**HABITAT** Prefers woodland, hedgerows and bushes. Often seen in parks and gardens.
**NESTING** 4-6 pale blue eggs, spotted with brown, are laid in a nest built next to tree trunk.
**RANGE** Widespread across Britain and western Europe; birds in northern and eastern Europe migrate south during the winter.

# REDWING (TURDUS ILIACUS)

**Voice** A weak, fluting song and a high-pitched call.

**Habitat** Generally found near hedgerows, in orchards and near pastureland, with breeding birds in Scotland found in conifer plantations.

**Nesting** Tree nests contain 4-6 blue eggs speckled with brown.

**Range** Breeds in northern Europe, including Iceland and Scandinavia with birds wintering in western Europe, including Britain.

Britain's smallest thrush, at rest the redwing looks very similar to the song thrush. It has warm brown upper parts and white underparts heavily marked with black spots. Unlike its relative, the redwing has a white stripe above the eye, extending from the bill to the back of the head. It also has chestnut-red patches on its flank. In flight, its distinctive red underwing can be clearly seen. It has a pale bill with a black tip and flesh-coloured legs. A countryside bird, the redwing is rarely seen in urban gardens. Length: 20-21cm.

# (TURDUS VISCIVORUS) MISTLE THRUSH

The mistle thrush is a large and powerful thrush, with a long tail and long wings. It is grey-brown above, with white edges to its flight feathers. Its underparts are white with large and distinctive black spots extending from its throat to its belly. Its long, square-ended tail is grey, with a white tip which can help with identification. Its face is mottled grey and its eyes and bill are dark. In flight, the underwings are white. The juvenile has a paler head and white spots on its upper parts. Length: 26-27cm.

**VOICE** A loud, shrill, warbling song.
**HABITAT** Prefers open woodland with large trees; can be found in parks and gardens.
**NESTING** A large nest in tree branches holds 4-5 pale blue eggs, spotted with brown.
**RANGE** Widespread across western and central Europe and found across Britain throughout the year.

# GARDEN WARBLER (SYLVIA BORIN)

**VOICE** A sweet, warbling song.
**HABITAT** Prefers mature and open woodland, with plenty of clearings. Also found in scrub, thickets and hedgerows.
**NESTING** Lays 4-5 white, buff-blotched eggs in a cup built into a bush.
**RANGE** Breeds across Europe and winters in Africa.

The garden warbler is a plump warbler, with a round head and a stubby bill. Its upper parts are a uniform olive-grey colour with slightly darker feathers on the wing tips and it has buff-coloured underparts. As the summer progresses, its plumage becomes more grey. Its dark eye is faintly ringed with white. It has stocky, blue-grey legs and a square-ended tail. Despite its name, it is not really a garden bird, preferring dense woodland to open gardens.
Length: 14cm.

# (ACROCEPHALUS SCHOENOBAENUS) SEDGE WARBLER

A small, plump warbler with a slightly flat head. The sedge warbler's upper parts are a warm brown colour, with dark streaks. Its crown is finely streaked with black and it has a distinctive broad creamy stripe above its eye with a fine black streak running across the eye below. Its underparts are white, with buff flanks. In flight, it shows a noticeably unstreaked rump and relatively more pointed wings than other warblers. Length: 13cm.

**VOICE** Its song, occasionally heard in flight, is sweet, warbling and trilling.

**HABITAT** Often found in dense undergrowth near to water such as reed beds, but also thickets and bushes.

**NESTING** 3-5 spotted green eggs are laid in a cup amongst reeds or sedges.

**RANGE** A summer visitor to most of western and central Europe, birds migrate to Africa.

# DARTFORD WARBLER
## (SYLVIA UNDATA)

The Dartford warbler is a small, dark warbler with short, rounded wings and a long tail that is frequently cocked. The plumage on its upper parts is a dark grey-brown. The male has deep red underparts with the exception of a white belly and undertail. It also has fine white spots on its chin. Its brown tail is tipped with white and it has pinkish legs. Its dark eye is surrounded by a red ring. The female is paler than the male. Length: 13cm.

**VOICE** A harsh, buzzing call and a metallic, warbling song.
**HABITAT** Prefers dry gorseland and heaths when in Britain.
**NESTING** Lays 3-4 white eggs with dark speckles in a ground cup hidden in vegetation.
**RANGE** Mainly found in the very south of Britain, it is resident in northern France, Spain and northern Africa.

# WOOD WARBLER (PHYLLOSCOPUS SIBILATRIX)

**VOICE** A clicking song which becomes a rapid trill.

**HABITAT** As its name suggests, it prefers woodland, mainly deciduous, with little or no ground cover.

**NESTING** Nests are built on the ground under the shelter of fallen branches or at the base of trees, and contain 6-7 white eggs speckled with brown.

**RANGE** Breeds across central and eastern Europe, with birds migrating to Africa.

Although a medium-sized warbler, the wood warbler is the largest of the leaf warbler variety, with a compact body, long wings and a short tail. Its upper parts are a bright yellow-green, and its throat is pure yellow. It has white underparts, gradually turning yellow on the breast. It also has a distinctive yellow eyebrow stripe above its dark eye. Its legs are a pale flesh colour. Length: 12-13cm.

# (PHYLLOSCOPUS TROCHILUS) WILLOW WARBLER

The willow warbler is a small and slim warbler with relatively longer wings. Its plumage is more defined and 'fresh' than that of the very similar chiffchaff. It has olive-brown upper parts, and during the spring and early summer its underparts are yellow. As the summer progresses its plumage becomes less bright. There is a marked pale eyebrow stripe and a dark stripe that runs through the eye. Its legs are usually pinkish, although some have darker legs, like those of the chiffchaff. Length: 10-11cm.

**Voice** A descending warble ending with a flourish.

**Habitat** Often found in young woodland and plantations or on the edges of woods where there is plenty of scrub.

**Nesting** Lays 6-7 white, red-spotted eggs in a domed ground nest.

**Range** Breeds across northern Europe from Britain and France to Scandinavia and Russia. Winters in Africa.

# REED WARBLER

## (ACROCEPHALUS SCIRPACEUS)

A small, brown warbler, the reed warbler is often mistaken for the very similar marsh warbler which is rare in Britain. Its head is flatter, with a sloping forehead, and it has relatively short wings. It has unstreaked, warm brown plumage on its back and upper wings, with a brown crown and tail. In flight it shows a chestnut rump. Its underparts are creamy white and it has a pure white throat. It has a slender, sharp bill and relatively dark legs. Towards late summer, its plumage becomes duller. Length: 13cm.

**VOICE** A repetitive chattering and trilling song that lacks melody.
**HABITAT** Prefers reed beds, although it can be found in orchards or farmland among tall vegetation.
**NESTING** Lays 4-5 pale green, olive-blotched eggs in a cup in reeds.
**RANGE** Found across central Europe during the summer, although absent from north; migrates to Africa.

# WHITETHROAT
(SYLVIA COMMUNIS)

The whitethroat is a common, medium-sized warbler with a relatively long tail. Its head and back are grey-brown and it has rust-coloured wings. The grey tail is also edged with white. Its underparts are a pinkish-buff colour except for its white throat which can be puffed out. Towards the end of summer, the male's plumage becomes much duller, whereas the female is less colourful throughout the year. Both have pinkish legs and a pale bill. A bolder warbler, it can often be seen flitting from bush to bush.
Length: 14cm.

**VOICE** A harsh call and a scratchy, warbling song.
**HABITAT** Prefers bushes, brambles, nettles and scrub and can be found near woodland.
**NESTING** 4-5 pale green, olive-speckled eggs are laid in a cup among bushes.
**RANGE** Breeds across Europe, winters in Africa.

# BLACKCAP (SYLVIA ATRICAPILLA)

**VOICE** A fluting, warbling song.
**HABITAT** Prefers woodland with plenty of
dense undergrowth, thickets and
bushes.
**NESTING** Lays 5 white eggs spotted with
brown in a cup built into a bush.
**RANGE** Found across Europe, with birds
from the north and the east
migrating to Africa. Most British birds
are resident throughout the year.

A larger, more stocky warbler with grey
plumage and distinctive markings on the
head. The male blackcap has grey-brown
plumage on its upper parts with pale grey
underparts. As the name suggests, it has a
black cap; this does not extend below the
eye and its face and the back of its neck are
grey. The female has paler plumage, with
rather more buff-coloured underparts; her
cap is chestnut-red. Both have grey faces,
brown eyes and pale legs. Length: 14-15cm.

# (PHYLLOSCOPUS COLLYBITA) CHIFFCHAFF

The chiffchaff is a small, compact bird with a round head, short wings and a long tail. It has olive-brown upper parts with a hint of yellow. Its underparts are pale buff in colour, which becomes yellower during the autumn when the bird's plumage is generally brighter. There is a pale stripe above the eye and a dark smudge running through it. The chiffchaff is very similar to its relative the willow warbler, but can be distinguished by its more muted colour and its dark legs. Length: 10-11cm.

**VOICE** A repeated 'chiff chaff' song.

**HABITAT** Prefers woodland and copses, with plenty of open ground and dense undergrowth. Can occasionally be seen in parks and gardens.

**NESTING** Nests are built either on the ground or low in the branches of bushes and contain 4-9 white eggs with dark speckles.

**RANGE** Found across Europe with eastern and northern birds migrating south towards Africa. Many of Britain's birds are resident throughout the year.

# GOLDCREST (REGULUS REGULUS)

**Voice** A high-pitched, warbling song.
**Habitat** Prefers coniferous forests, although can be found in deciduous woods, parks and gardens.
**Nesting** A cup is woven on the high branches of a conifer and contains 7-10 white eggs, speckled with brown.
**Range** Resident throughout the year in western and central Europe.

Britain and Europe's smallest bird, the goldcrest is a round-bodied, short-tailed warbler. The plumage on its back and tail is olive-green and its wings are blackish with two bold white wing bars. Its underparts are buff-white with a yellow wash on the flanks. Its most distinctive feature is the yellow (female) or orange (male) patch on the top of its head which is bordered with black. Juvenile birds lack the colourful crest. Its face is plain, with a very faint moustachial streak at the base of the short, dark bill.
Length: 9cm.

# (REGULUS IGNICAPILLUS) FIRECREST

Similar in size and appearance to the goldcrest, the firecrest is slightly larger with a less rounded shape. It has brighter, yellow-green upper parts, with a slightly bronzed wash on the sides of the neck and 'shoulders'. Its underparts are white. There are two white wing bars on the dark wings. The male has a deep orange stripe on its crown and the female a yellow one; both have a broad black border to the crest. There is a further white eyebrow stripe and a dark stripe running through the eye. Juvenile birds lack the crest but have the striped head markings.
Length: 9cm.

**VOICE** A high-pitched 'zi zi zi' call.
**HABITAT** Found in conifer forests and plantations although some do inhabit deciduous woodland with plenty of bushes and shrubs.
**NESTING** Lays 7-11 white, brown-speckled eggs in a cup suspended on branches.
**RANGE** Breeds across western and central Europe with eastern birds migrating south.

# SPOTTED FLYCATCHER (MUSCICAPA STRIATA)

**VOICE** A weak but harsh 'twee' call.

**HABITAT** Prefers open areas close to or in woodland, such as glades and forest edges. Can be found in parks and gardens.

**NESTING** Lays 4-5 pale blue, brown-blotched eggs in a tree nest.

**RANGE** A common summer visitor across Europe; migrates to tropical Africa.

The spotted flycatcher is a small bird with a rounded head, short legs and a relatively broad and flat dark bill. It has typically long wings and tail. The upper parts are a pale grey-brown colour and its wing feathers are edged with buff-white. The crown of the head is whitish, marked with delicate darker stripes. The underparts are a dirty white with dark streaks on the breast, fading to white on the belly and undertail. Juvenile birds are similar colours but with distinctive spots, which give them a scaly appearance. The spotted flycatcher sits very upright on its perch and, when it flies, moves erratically in pursuit of its prey before returning, often to the same perch.
Length: 14-15cm.

# (FICEDULA HYPOLEUCA) PIED FLYCATCHER

Smaller than the spotted flycatcher, the pied flycatcher has a flatter head and a shorter tail. During spring and summer the adult male has black and white pied markings. Its upper parts are sooty black, with a white patch on the wing and another on the base of the bill that does not stretch as far as the eyes. Its underparts are white, including white plumage on the underside of the tail. It has dark legs, black eyes and a relatively broad and short black bill. In winter the male's plumage turns brown, with buff feathers on the chest and belly. The female is brown throughout the year, with similar markings to the male. The juvenile is also brown pied, with spotting above and speckles below. Length: 13cm.

**VOICE** A sharp 'wic' call and a trilling song.

**HABITAT** Found in mixed woodland although prefers deciduous trees for nesting. Can often be seen in parks and gardens, particularly near rivers and streams.

**NESTING** Lays 5-7 blue eggs in a nest built into a tree hole.

**RANGE** A summer visitor to central and eastern Europe and some parts of Spain and France. Winters in western Africa.

# GREAT TIT
## (PARUS MAJOR)

A large, stocky tit, the great tit is the biggest member of the tit family. Its back is olive green and its wings and tail are a blue-grey. It has a black cap which runs into a black collar. Its cheeks are white and its throat is black, extending down the breast and belly in a broad stripe. In males, the stripe widens at the legs, in females it is a uniform width. The underparts are pale yellow. Its eye and bill are black and its legs are dark grey. Juveniles are paler versions of the adults. Length: 13-15cm.

**VOICE** A variety of loud calls.
**HABITAT** Prefers deciduous woodland although can be found in conifer plantations. Often seen in hedgerows, parks and gardens where there are trees.
**NESTING** Nests are built into tree holes or crevices and contain 5-12 white eggs with red spots.
**RANGE** Found across Europe throughout the year, with the exception of Iceland and northern Scandinavia.

# LONG-TAILED TIT
## (AEGITHALOS CAUDATUS)

As its name suggests, this bird has a proportionally long tail. The long-tailed tit's body is small and rounded and it has short, rounded wings. Its plumage is a mixture of pink, brown and white, with pinkish-brown upper parts and pinkish-white underparts. Its crown is black, with a broad white stripe running through it. Its brown-black wing feathers are edged with white and its black tail has distinctive white edges. Some subspecies have a completely white head and whiter underparts. Its eyes and tiny bill are black and its legs are dark. Length: 14-15cm.

**VOICE** A rattling trill and a high-pitched call.
**HABITAT** Often found at the edge of deciduous woodland, in bushier places such as hedgerows and scrub. Can be seen in parks and gardens.
**NESTING** Lays 8-12 white eggs in a domed nest bound with cobwebs, built into a bramble thicket or bush.
**RANGE** Found across Europe throughout the year, with the exception of Iceland and northern Scandinavia.

# WILLOW TIT (PARUS MONTANUS)

**VOICE** A nasal, grating call and a rarely heard warbling song.

**HABITAT** Found in damp woodland, close to water. Not often found in gardens.

**NESTING** 6-9 white, red-speckled eggs are laid in a tree hole excavated by the bird, usually from rotten wood.

**RANGE** Found across central and eastern Europe throughout the year. Rare in Ireland and Scotland.

The willow tit is a small bird with a rounded head, short, rounded wings and a proportionally longish tail. It has a slightly scruffy appearance. It has brown upper parts, with a dark, almost black cap stretching to the back of the neck. Its underparts are a dirty white with buff plumage on the flanks. Its face is white, contrasting sharply with the black cap, and it has a small black bib on its throat which fades into the white breast. It has dark legs, black eyes and a short black bill.
Length: 11-12cm.

# (PARUS PALUSTRIS) MARSH TIT

Very similar in appearance to the willow tit, the marsh tit is a small, compact bird with a short neck and short, rounded wings. Its upper parts are plain brown and it is dirty white below with rather more buff-coloured flanks. It has a glossy black crown, unlike the scruffy crown of the willow tit. Its cheeks are white and it has a small black bib below its bill. Its black markings are clearly defined and smaller than those of its relative. Its eyes and bill are black and its legs are dark.
Length: 11-12cm.

**VOICE** A clear, loud call and a chirping and trilling song.

**HABITAT** Found in deciduous woodland and any environment with plenty of trees nearby. Can be seen in parks and gardens.

**NESTING** Lays 7-8 white eggs in a tree hole lined with moss and hair.

**RANGE** Found in central and eastern Europe throughout the year. Rarely seen in Scotland and Ireland.

# CRESTED TIT (PARUS CRISTATUS)

**VOICE** A high-pitched, trilling call.
**HABITAT** An arboreal bird, in Britain it
is found only in Scots pine forests in
the Highlands. Elsewhere it can be
found in more mixed woodland.
**NESTING** Lays 4-8 purple-spotted eggs
in a hole in a rotten tree excavated
by the female.
**RANGE** Found across conifer forests in
Europe throughout the year.

As its name suggests, the crested tit is
distinctive because of its crest. Its upper
parts are a plain brown and it is white below
with buff-coloured flanks. Its face is a
greyish white and separated from the body
by a thin black collar. It also has a thin black
eye strip that curves back across the cheek.
At the nape of the neck the collar broadens
and it has a black bib at the throat. Its crest
is marked with black and white bars which
give it a scaly appearance. It has a dark bill,
grey legs and dark orange eyes.
Length: 11-12cm.

# (PARUS ATER) COAL TIT

A very small tit, with a rounded body and a relatively short tail. The coal tit's back, wings and tail are grey and its underparts are white, with buff-coloured flanks. It has a black head with white cheeks and a black throat. There is a distinctive white stripe running down the back of the head to the nape of the neck. The coal tit also has small white wing bars, easily seen when at rest. Juvenile birds have similar markings to the adult, but instead of white plumage they have yellow, including the wing bars. Coal tits can be seen searching for food on tree trunks and branches, often hanging upside down. Length: 10-12cm.

**VOICE** A variety of high-pitched calls.

**HABITAT** Prefers coniferous woodland and plantations, but can be found in mixed woods. Often seen in parks and gardens.

**NESTING** Leaves 7-10 red-spotted, white eggs in a moss-lined tree hole.

**RANGE** Abundant throughout Europe, although only a winter visitor in some parts of France and Italy.

# BLUE TIT
(PARUS CAERULEUS)

A common and frequent garden visitor, the blue tit is a small compact tit. Its back is olive green and its wings and tail are a bright blue. There is a small pale bar on the wings and its breast and belly are yellow. It has a blue crown which can be raised to form a small crest. Its cheeks are white and bordered with a thin black collar which meets the black 'chin'. It also has a distinctive black eye stripe which extends to the dark nape. The blue tit has dark eyes, a dark bill and blue legs. Length: 11-12cm.

**VOICE** Its call is a high-pitched 'tsee tsee tsee tsu'.
**HABITAT** Although found in a variety of habitats, it prefers deciduous woodland. Often seen in parks and gardens where it feeds in bushes and trees.
**NESTING** Lays 7-14 white, brown-spotted eggs in a moss and feather-lined tree hole.
**RANGE** Abundant across Europe throughout the year.

# BEARDED TIT (PANURUS BIARMICUS)

**VOICE** A repeated, metallic call.
**HABITAT** Found in reed beds where it feeds on insects and seeds.
**NESTING** Lays 5-7 white eggs with brown streaks in an open reed nest laid on ground or in vegetation.
**RANGE** Found across Europe in areas with suitable habitat. Birds in Britain remain throughout the year.

A small bird, the bearded tit has a long tail, short, rounded wings and is larger in size than the long-tailed tit. Its upper parts and flanks are a gingery brown colour and it has a white breast and belly. The male has a pale blue-grey head with a conspicuous black moustache extending down below the eye. The female's head is plain brown. The bearded tit's tail is edged with white and its wings are marked with white and black streaks. It has a small orange bill, orange eyes and black legs. Juvenile birds have a dark streak down the centre of the back. Length: 16-17cm.

# (SITTA EUROPAEA) NUTHATCH

The nuthatch is a small bird with a long, straight bill, short neck, wings and tail. It has blue-grey upper parts and white underparts becoming chestnut on the flanks and under the tail. Its cheeks are white and it has a long, dark streak running through the eye to the back of the head. In flight, its broad wings are rounded. It has a square-ended tail, tipped with white, dark eyes, a grey bill with a black tip and orange legs. Length: 13-14cm.

**VOICE** A high-pitched, ringing call.
**HABITAT** Found in mature, deciduous woodland, parks and gardens.
**NESTING** Lays 6-11 white eggs with red spots in a tree hole sealed with mud to keep out intruders.
**RANGE** Found throughout Europe except in the far north, including Scotland, Iceland and Scandinavia.

# TREECREEPER (CERTHIA FAMILIARIS)

**VOICE** A thin, high-pitched call with a jumble of notes.

**HABITAT** Found in woodland of all types and sizes. Can be seen in parks and gardens, in both trees and hedges.

**NESTING** Lays 6 white eggs with red and brown spots in a twig nest built into tree trunk.

**RANGE** Found across central and eastern Europe, although limited in France and Spain.

The treecreeper is a small arboreal bird with a short neck, long, curved bill and long, pointed tail. Its plumage above is brown, marked with streaks and spots. Its underparts are white with a brown rump. In flight its wings are long, broad and rounded and show a distinctive pale wing bar. It also has a pale 'eyebrow' stripe above the eye. As its name suggests, the treecreeper works its way up the trunk of a tree in search of food and its plumage provides excellent camouflage. Its long, downward-curving bill and long toes are also distinctive features. Length: 12-13cm.

# (GARRULUS GLANDARIUS) JAY

A large bird, although smaller than a magpie. The plumage on the jay's back and underparts is a pinkish-brown, and it has a white rump and a long black tail. Its head is topped with a white crown, marked with black streaks, which can be raised into a small crest. There is also a black moustache streak running down from the bill, below the eye to the white chin. Its wings are black with a white patch; there is another patch of blue at the 'elbow' which is marked with thin black streaks. These markings are most easily seen when the bird is in flight. Its bill is dark and its eyes are pale blue. Length: 33-35cm.

**Voice** A harsh, screeching call.

**Habitat** A woodland bird, can be found amongst or near trees of any type. Often seen in parks and gardens where there are mature trees.

**Nesting** Lays 5-7 pale green eggs with dark spots in a stick nest high in a tree.

**Range** Found across Europe throughout the year.

# MAGPIE
## (PICA PICA)

The magpie is a very
common and easily
recognized pied bird, a
medium-sized member of
the crow family with a
round head, sturdy body,
long legs and a long tail. Its
head and body are mainly
black, except for its white
belly which contrasts
sharply with the black breast
band. Its wings are black
with white 'shoulders' and
white feathers on the outer
wing, which are edged with
black. The wings and the
black tail have an iridescent
green sheen. The eyes, bill
and legs are black.
Length: 44-48cm.

**Voice** A rattling chatter and
occasionally a quiet, bubbling
song.
**Habitat** Prefers trees, hedges,
thickets and occasionally man-
made structures such as pylons.
**Nesting** 5-8 green, brown-spotted
eggs are laid in a domed stick
nest placed in a tall tree.
**Range** Found across Europe
throughout the year, except in
mountainous regions.

# JACKDAW (CORVUS MONEDULA)

**Voice** A high-pitched, yelping 'chack' and a cawing 'kaa'.

**Habitat** Found in a variety of habitats, from open woodland and farmland to gardens, churches and cliff tops.

**Nesting** Lays 4-6 pale blue, black-spotted eggs in a stick nest, built into the side of a tree, building or cliff.

**Range** Found across Europe throughout the year, from southern Scandinavia to Spain.

The smallest member of the crow family, the jackdaw is quite stocky with a short, black bill. Its plumage is completely black with a slightly purple sheen on the head and back. The nape of its neck is a dark grey, which is paler and more obvious in the female. In flight, its long, broad wings are rounded and the feathers are 'fingered' at the ends. Its eyes are grey and its bill and legs are black. A sociable bird, it can often be seen in flocks performing aerobatics. Length: 32-34cm.

# (CORVUS FRUGILEGUS) ROOK

Slightly smaller than the crow, the rook has a steep forehead and a straight, pointed bill. Its plumage is glossy black with a purplish sheen and its grey bill has a patch of grey skin at the base. In flight, its wings are straight, broad and 'fingered' at the ends. The feathers around the top of its legs are shaggy and its crown feathers also stand up when it is excited. A gregarious and social bird, the rook roosts in large numbers and can often be seen squabbling over territory. Length: 44-46cm

**VOICE** A cawing call.

**HABITAT** Prefers tall trees and may be seen in farmland, copses and open woodland. Can also be seen in urban areas.

**NESTING** Lays 3-5 pale green eggs in a nest of sticks and earth built into the top of a tree. Nests in colonies.

**RANGE** Found across Europe; northern birds migrate to southern areas during the winter.

# CARRION CROW (CORVUS CORONE CORONE)

**Voice** A deep cawing call.

**Habitat** A variety of habitats, from open farmland and moorland, coasts and sea cliffs to busy urban areas.

**Nesting** Lays 4-6 blue or green eggs with brown spots in a stick and mud nest built into a tree top or onto a cliff ledge.

**Range** Both subspecies are found across Europe throughout the year.

There two subspecies of crow: the carrion crow, which is all black, and the hooded crow, which has a grey body, black head, wings and tail. Both have a heavy black bill with thick plumage at the base. In flight their wings are long and broad with 'fingered' feathers at the tips and their tails have square ends. The carrion crow's forehead is flatter than the rook's. They fly with slowly flapped wings and are less aerobatic than their relatives.

Length: 45-47cm.

# (CORVUS CORAX) RAVEN

The largest member of the crow family, the raven is powerfully built with a large bill, flat head, long neck and long wings. It is all black with a purple sheen when seen in the right light. It has loose feathers on its throat which can look quite scruffy. In flight, its broad wings are angular and its tail has a wedge shape; it tumbles, glides and soars, and frequently performs aerobatics. It can also be seen walking on the ground, often rather majestically. Ravens will eat almost anything, including carrion; they may also kill small animals. Length: 63-64cm.

**VOICE** A loud and deep croaking call.

**HABITAT** Usually found near mountains and cliffs, but will also nest on suitable buildings and in dense woodland.

**NESTING** Large stick nests are built on ledges or in trees and contain 4-6 light blue or green eggs with dark brown spots.

**RANGE** Found across most of Europe although absent from eastern Britain and parts of France and Germany.

# STARLING
## (STURNUS VULGARIS)

A medium-sized bird with a plump body, a long bill and a short tail. The starling's plumage is very dark, almost black with a purple and green sheen in summer. The upper parts are marked with brown spots, and the underparts are plain. During the winter it becomes heavily spotted with white all over its body. In summer its bill is yellow, turning dark during the winter. Brown winter legs and feet become pink during the early summer. In flight, its wings are short, with a broad base and a pointed end, giving a triangular overall shape; it has a square-ended tail. Juvenile birds are an unspotted grey. Often seen in large flocks performing aerobatic displays. Length: 21-22cm.

**VOICE** A variety of calls and songs. Often mimics the songs of other birds and even the sound of car alarms.

**HABITAT** Found in a range of habitats; prefers open countryside for feeding but will also frequent parks, gardens, rubbish tips and man-made structures.

**NESTING** Lays 5-7 pale blue eggs in a lined hole in a tree or building.

**RANGE** Found throughout Europe. Birds in northern regions migrate south, to Spain and Africa.

# HOUSE SPARROW
## (PASSER DOMESTICUS)

The house sparrow is a small, plump bird with a round head and a short, thick bill. Its upper parts are chestnut brown with dark streaks on the back and wings. The male has a grey crown, bordered with brown, and a black patch on its throat. It also has grey underparts and a grey rump. The female has a brown crown and pale, buffy underparts; she lacks the grey rump. She also has a pale streak above the eyes. Both sexes have a small white wing bar. The dark bill becomes black during the breeding season. Length: 14-15cm.

**VOICE** Chirping and cheeping calls.
**HABITAT** Prefers cultivated land near to human habitation, such as parks, gardens, fields and hedges.
**NESTING** An untidy straw nest is built into a building or bush and contains 3-5 white eggs with grey blotches.
**RANGE** Widespread across Europe and Asia.

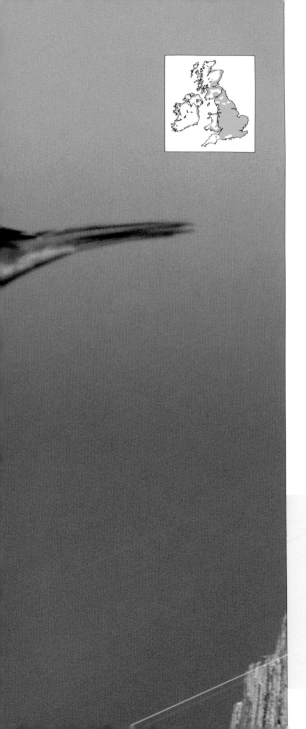

# TREE SPARROW
## (PASSER MONTANUS)

The tree sparrow is a small and compact bird with a short neck, round head and a sleeker body than the house sparrow. Its upper parts are chestnut brown, streaked with black, and it has a chestnut crown. Its underparts are dirty white, washed with buff on the flanks, with a yellow-brown rump. It has white cheeks and a white collar, broken at the front by a black bib. It also has a distinctive black patch in the centre of its cheek. Both sexes are alike and do not change colour with the seasons. Length: 13-15cm.

**VOICE** High-pitched chirps and cheeps.
**HABITAT** Prefers woodland and hedgerows and can often be seen on agricultural land and in parks and gardens.
**NESTING** Builds nest into a tree hole and lays 4-6 white eggs blotched with brown and grey.
**RANGE** Found across Europe throughout the year, although rare in Ireland and Scotland.

# CHAFFINCH
## (FRINGILLA COELEBS)

A small, plump bird with a thick neck, long wings and long tail. The chaffinch has a brown back and a grey head and its tail is brown with white edging. Its rump is olive green. Its cheeks and underparts are pinkish brown, with the male displaying much brighter colours than the female. In flight, its black-brown wings are clearly marked with a broad white wing bar and white 'shoulder' patches. Its medium-sized bill and legs are grey and its eyes are black. Length: 14-15cm.

**VOICE** A loud, 'pink' call and a warbling song.

**HABITAT** Prefers woodland for nesting, but can also be seen in hedgerows, on farmland and in parks and gardens.

**NESTING** Lays 4-5 blue-green eggs with purple streaks in a neat nest built into a tree or bush.

**RANGE** Found across Europe with northern birds migrating south towards North Africa.

# BRAMBLING (FRINGILLA MONTIFRINGILLA)

**VOICE** A nasal call and a rarely heard, wheezing song.

**HABITAT** Usually seen in woodland with plenty of food, particularly beech woods. Sometimes seen in gardens.

**NESTING** Tree nests contain 5-7 light blue eggs with dark streaks.

**RANGE** Breeds in Scandinavia and Russia and moves into southern areas of Europe for the winter.

The brambling is similar in size and shape to its relative the chaffinch, but with a forked tail. A winter visitor to Britain, the male and female are alike at that time. It has brown and black upper parts with orange markings on the wings. Its rump is a distinctive white and its underparts are dirty white with an orange-buff breast and shoulder. In flight, its long, broad wings show two white wing bars and a white patch. Its eyes and stubby bill are black. During the summer, the male's upper parts become black. Length: 14cm.

# (CARDUELIS CHLORIS) GREENFINCH

A chunky finch, the greenfinch has a large head and a relatively short tail. The male has green upper parts with a yellow-green rump, and its underparts are yellowish. Its wings have yellow patches on the forward feathers, which show as bright streaks when the bird is at rest. The female is duller than the male and lacks the bright yellow markings; she has brown streaks on her upper parts and flanks. The greenfinch has a conical bill and pinkish legs. It can often be seen in small flocks or perched high in branches, singing.
Length: 14-15cm.

**VOICE** A nasal call and a twittering song.

**HABITAT** Woodland edges, copses, hedgerows, churchyards and farmland are favoured. Can be seen in parks and gardens.

**NESTING** Bulky twig nests are built into trees or hedges and contain 4-6 pale blue eggs with brown markings.

**RANGE** Found throughout Europe, with northern birds heading towards southern coasts for the winter.

# GOLDFINCH
## (CARDUELIS CARDUELIS)

A slimmer and more dainty-looking finch than its relatives, the goldfinch has a round head and a slightly forked tail. Its upper parts are brown, with a white rump and a black tail, edged with white. Its underparts are white, with a buff-brown wash on the flanks. It has a distinctive head, with a red face bordered on the sides and throat with white. Its crown is also red, and the back of its head and the nape of the neck are black. Its black eye is surrounded by a black streak. In flight, its black wings are marked with a broad yellow wing bar which is also conspicuous when the bird is at rest. Its bill is pink with a dark tip and its legs are yellow.
Length: 12-13cm.

**VOICE** A tinkling call and a twittering song.
**HABITAT** Found on open ground, woodland edges, near bushes and hedges. Often seen in parks and gardens.
**NESTING** Lays 4-7 black-speckled, blue eggs in a cup nest in a bush.
**RANGE** Found throughout Europe, with northern birds heading south for the winter.

# LINNET (ACANTHIS CANNABINA)

**VOICE** A high-pitched, rapid twittering.
**HABITAT** Prefers low bushes, gorseland, scrub and hedgerows.
**NESTING** Lays 4-6 red-speckled, blue eggs in a cup nest placed in a bush.
**RANGE** Found across western and central Europe throughout the year. Summer visitor to eastern Europe and Russia.

The linnet is a slender finch with a forked tail. It has an unstreaked, rich brown back and tail. The male has a grey head with a chestnut-red forehead and breast. The underparts are buff, fading to white, and it also has a white throat with dark streaks. The female lacks the red markings and is streaked with dark brown. The wings are brown and black and it has white edges to its flight feathers. The tail is also edged with white. It has dark eyes, a short, grey bill and grey legs. Length: 13-14cm.

# (CARDUELIS SPINUS) SISKIN

A small finch, with a relatively shorter, forked tail and a long, slender bill. The male siskin has an olive-green back, heavily streaked with black. Its underparts are green-yellow fading to white on the belly and undertail, streaked with black. Its rump is yellow and the sides of its black tail are also yellow. It has a black crown and a small black bib which varies in size. Its wings are black and yellow and in flight it shows yellow wing bars. The female is very similar to the male, but less yellow with a streaky crown. Length: 12-13cm.

**VOICE** A nasal call and a twittering song.

**HABITAT** Found in forests and woodland, where it breeds. Can be seen in parks and gardens.

**NESTING** Lays 3-5 pale blue eggs with red spots in a nest built into tree a top.

**RANGE** Found across Europe; breeds in northern areas and winters towards Mediterranean.

# REDPOLL (CARDUELIS FLAMMEA)

**Voice** A nasal, trilling call.

**Habitat** Prefers heaths and woodland, but in Britain can often be seen at coastal sites before continuing migration westwards.

**Nesting** Lays 4-5 blue eggs with brown spots in a twig nest built into a tree or bush.

**Range** Found across central and eastern Europe, breeding in the north, with some birds moving into southern areas.

A small finch with a rounded body and a forked tail. The redpoll's plumage is heavily streaked with dark brown on white, and a darker effect above. It has a red forehead and a black chin. Its rump is white and it also has white bars on its wings. During the breeding season the male's chest and rump become rose pink, whereas the female's breast is streaked like the rest of her body. Different subspecies vary in the intensity of their streaking. It has a dark eye, a short yellow bill and black legs. Length: 12-13cm.

# (PYRRHULA PYRRHULA) BULLFINCH

The bullfinch is a chunky finch with a short, thick neck and a large head. Its upper parts are mainly grey, with a black crown and nape and black wings. Its tail is a glossy black and it has a white rump which is most conspicuous in flight. Its underparts and shoulders are pink, brighter in the male and greyer in the female. Its face and chin are pure black. There is a broad white wing bar, obvious both in flight and at rest. It has a short, sturdy black bill, and black eyes and legs. Length: 13-15cm.

**Voice** A low, soft call.
**Habitat** Prefers woodland, hedges and thickets. Can be seen in parks and gardens.
**Nesting** Lays 4-5 light blue eggs with dark brown spots in a nest built into a bush or hedge.
**Range** Found across Europe throughout the year, with some northern birds migrating south.

# HAWFINCH (COCCOTHRAUSTES COCCOTHRAUSTES)

**VOICE** A 'tic tic' call.

**HABITAT** Prefers deciduous and mixed woodland; can also be found in urban areas with trees, including parks and gardens.

**NESTING** Lays 5 pale blue eggs with dark streaks in a cup placed in a tree or shrub.

**RANGE** Found across Europe throughout the year, with northern and eastern birds heading for the Mediterranean in winter.

A large and sturdy finch with a very large bill, a large head, thick neck and short tail. Both the male and female hawfinch are brown above and pinkish-brown below. The hawfinch has an orange-brown head with a black border around the thick-based bill and a black bib. A grey collar separates the head from the back. Its wings are black with white patches and brown 'shoulders'. Its square-ended tail is brown, with a white end. The bill is grey-blue in the summer, turning to dull yellow for the winter. Length: 16-18cm.

# (LOXIA CURVIROSTRA) COMMON CROSSBILL

The common crossbill is the only British bird which has the tips of its bill crossed, enabling it to pick seeds out of cones. The bill is large and heavy-looking, and a grey-brown colour; it is proportionally large. Males vary in colour from orange-red to green; juveniles are duller and rather more streaked. Females are green-grey with a yellow-green rump; both sexes have dark brown wings and tails. The crossbill can be seen in conifers edging sideways along branches, moving rather like a parrot. Length: 16-17cm.

**Voice** Twittering song; 'jip jip' call.

**Habitat** Coniferous forest, especially spruce and fir.

**Nesting** Timing is linked to a crop of cones. A grass-lined nest built high in a conifer; lays 3-4 green eggs with purple-red blotches.

**Range** Northern Europe across into Russia. Present all year in Scotland; summer 'irruptions' into Britain from across North Sea may be linked to shortage of food.

# YELLOWHAMMER (EMBERIZA CITRINELLA)

**VOICE** A nasal call, which is often rendered as 'little-bit-of-bread-and-no-cheese'.

**HABITAT** Found on grassland, farmland and fields with hedges as well as embankments. Rarely seen in gardens.

**NESTING** Lays 3-5 white eggs with purple spots in a cup built into a bush.

**RANGE** Found across Europe throughout the year, with northern birds moving south during winter.

A long-bodied bunting with a long, forked tail. The male yellowhammer has a brown, streaky back with a chestnut rump. Its head is bright yellow as are its underparts. Its chest and belly are streaked with brown. The female is similarly marked but less brightly coloured and with more streaks. In flight, the yellowhammer shows two pale wing bars and its tail is edged with white. It has a small grey bill, dark eyes and grey legs.
Length: 16-17cm.

# (EMBERIZA SCHOENICLUS) REED BUNTING

The reed bunting is a small bird with a large, round head and sturdy body. Its upper parts are brown, streaked with black. Its white underparts are streaked on the flanks. The male has a black head and a black throat with a white moustache and a white collar. The female has a brown head with a pale brown 'eyebrow' stripe and a pale moustache extending to the neck collar. The male has a grey rump; the female's is brown. During the winter, the male's head and throat become mottled with brown. Length: 15-16cm.

**VOICE** A loud, grating call.
**HABITAT** Found in reed beds, on river banks, marshes and coastal sites. Can also be seen on drier farmland.
**NESTING** Lays 4-5 olive eggs in a grass nest placed on the ground in vegetation.
**RANGE** Found across Europe with birds in Scandinavia and Russia migrating towards the south west in winter.

# CORN BUNTING (MILIARIA CALANDRA)

**VOICE** A rattling and jangling song.

**HABITAT** Prefers open countryside and can usually be seen on grassland, farmland and rough, fallow fields.

**NESTING** A loose grass nest is hidden on the ground among grass or weeds and contains 4-6 light brown eggs with dark streaks and spots.

**RANGE** Found across Europe throughout the year, although restricted to the eastern and southern counties of England and Scotland.

The largest bunting in Britain, the corn bunting is plump with a large head and a short, stout bill. The plumage on its upper parts is grey-brown with heavy black streaks and its underparts are dirty white with finer brown streaks. Its stubby bill is a dull yellow colour; it has black eyes and pale, flesh-coloured legs. Males and females are similar. It can often be seen perched high up, singing with its head held back. In flight, it dangles its legs. Length: 18-20cm.

# (PLECTROPHENAX NIVALIS) SNOW BUNTING

The snow bunting is a chunky bunting with a thick bill, a flat head and a short, forked tail. It has a pure white body with a black back and large black tips on the wings. It also has a black stripe running up the centre of the tail. In winter, its back fades to brown with black streaks. During the autumn and winter, the male's white head and breast become a sandy colour, making it look similar to the female. The short, thick bill is dark in summer and orange-yellow in winter. In flight, its broad wings are triangular and pointed. A sociable bird, the snow bunting often forms very large flocks. Length: 16-17cm.

**VOICE** A loud twittering.

**HABITAT** Prefers open, stony country such as high tundra or mountains. British migrants can be seen on the seashore.

**NESTING** Lays 4-6 whitish eggs with brown spots in a nest concealed amongst stones.

**RANGE** Resident in Iceland and Scandinavia, with some birds also resident in the Scottish highlands. Some migrate towards eastern Europe.

# INDEX

# ACKNOWLEDGEMENTS

Illustrations

The publisher would like to thank Oxford Scientific/Photolibrary.com for providing the photographs for this book. We would also like to thank the following for their kind permission to reproduce their photographs:

16, 20/21, 26/27, 28, 44, 46/47, 48, 53, 58, 59, 67, 76/77, 78/79, 84, 86/87, 88, 90/91, 92, 99, 105, 108, 109, 110, 111, 113, 115, 122, 128/129, 138, 140/141, 146/147, 157, 165, 167, 173, 177, 178/9, 181, 182/183, 187 188, 190/191, 194, 197, 200, 201, 212/213, 214/215, 218, 219, 220/221, 223, 236/7, 238/239 (and back flap image), 241, 247, 250 Mark Hamblin; 17 Tony Martin; 18 Chris Perrins; 19, 184, 185 Jos Korenromp; 22, 23, 24/25, 126, 130, 133, 180, 211 Richard Packwood; 29, 202/203, 253 George Reszeter; 30/31 W Wisniewksi/Okapia; 32/33 Harold Taylor Abipp; 34 John Downer; 35, 38/39, 50/51, 52 Ian West; 36/37 Bill Pattern; 40, 117, 176 Barry Walker; 41, 80/81, 95, 100/101, 120, 121, 132, 158/159 (and front cover image), 189 and back cover image David Tipling; 42 Tony Allen; 43 T C Middleton; 45 David Boyle; 49, 74 Tony Bomford; 54/54 Edward Robinson; 56, 225 Niall Benvie; 57 OSF; 60 Adam Jones; 61 Tom Ulrich; 62 Konrad Wothe; 63 Daybreak Imagery; 64/65 Mike Birkhead; 66, 68/69, 104, 206, 240, 245 Chris Knights; 70/71 Eric Thielscher; 72/73, 123, 144 Eric Woods; 75 W Layer; 82/83, 148/149, 152,154/155,249 Michael Leach; 85, 152, 217 Irving Cushing; 93, 160 Alan Hartley; 94, 107, 112, 124, 166, 170, 172, 196, 198/199, 207, 216, 246, 248,251 Tony Tilford; 96/97, 127, 161, 224 D J Sanders; 98, 244 Frances Furlong; 102/103, 222, 234/235 Mike Powles; 106, 114, 162/163, 242/243 Carlos Sanchez Alonso; 116, 118/119,139 Kenneth Day; 131 Bill Paton; 135 Brian Kenney; 136 Stephen Mills; 137 Mike Powles; 142, 168/169, 192/193 Gordon Maclean; 143 Margot Conte; 145 Norbert Rosing; 150/151 Brand/Okapia; 153 Ken Cole; 171 Roy Coombes; 174/175, 186, 228 Keith Ringland; 195 Michael Richards; 204/205 Dennis Green; 208 Terry Heathcote; 210 Terry Andrewartha; 226/227 Ben Osborne; 229 Jim Hallett; 230 Hans Reinhard; 231 Doug Allen; 232/233, 252 Manfred Pfefferle; 134 Richard Vaughan/ardea.com; 209 R T Smith/ardea.com

With thanks to Glen Balmer, John Mackay,
Oliver Higgs, Kate Santon, Kate Truman, Angela Blackwood Murray,
Ruth Blair and everyone at Oxford Scientific Films.